DEATH

DEATH

corpses, cadavers, and other grave matters

Elizabeth A. Murray, PhD

 Twenty-First Century Books • Minneapolis

To my father, whose life and death taught me much about being human, and my mother, whose body will someday teach others about life. With love to my daughter-in-law, Mindy, whose gentle touch heals and nurtures. Most of all, I dedicate this book to my wonderful son, Tim Bucher, with whom I read countless children's stories, each of which ultimately concluded with the same phrase, "I sure do . . . love you."

Acknowledgments: Thank you to the Imbrogno family for the privileges extended during the passing of their parents. Much appreciation to two consummate readers—my sister, Kathy Isaacs, and friend Elizabeth Villing—for careful reviews of my first draft. I am grateful to Andrea Hatten, Dorothy Haynes, and Connie Kreyling for assistance in obtaining interviews. My best to colleagues entomologist Gene Kritsky and microbiologist Annette Muckerheide for expertise regarding "bugs" of all kinds. Thanks also to Domenica DiPiazza for this unique opportunity and to Marcia Marshall and Kellie Hultgren for all their help.

The image on page 2 and repeated throughout the book shows the bubble-shaped bacteria *Neisseria meningitidis,* which causes the disease meningococcal meningitis. If left untreated, this disease can cause brain damage, coma, and death.

Twenty-First Century Books
A division of Lerner Publishing Group, Inc.
241 First Avenue North
Minneapolis, MN 55401 U.S.A.

Website address: www.lernerbooks.com

Library of Congress Cataloging-in-Publication Data

Murray, Elizabeth A.
    Death : corpses, cadavers, and other grave matters by Elizabeth A. Murray.
        p.   cm. — (Discovery!)
    Includes bibliographical references and index.
    ISBN 978–0–7613–3851–2 (lib. bdg. : alk. paper)
    1. Death (Biology) 2. Postmortem changes. I. Title.
QP87.M92 2010
    616.07'59—dc22   2009017436

Manufactured in the United States of America
1 – JR – 12/15/09

CONTENTS

Chapter 1

MATTERS OF LIFE AND DEATH

Most of us easily recognize a living thing when we see it. Organisms that are alive share certain common features. These include growth and reproduction, responding to the surrounding environment and, in many cases, the ability to move. All living, healthy beings have chemical reactions going on inside them that maintain life. They are also able to regulate their bodily processes. All the chemical reactions happening within a living organism are known as its metabolism.

Nonliving things lack all or most of these traits. For example, a rock has none of the features common to life-forms. Clouds do move and even seem to grow, but they are not alive. Bubbles appear to reproduce when you shake soapy water, but bubbles are nonliving. Simply lacking the characteristics of life, however, does not define death. For something to be dead, it has to have once been alive.

Building a Living Body

The smallest unit of life is a single cell. All the traits of living things are present in cells. Cells reproduce by dividing. They interact with their surroundings. They undergo chemical reactions that keep them alive. Chemicals make up all parts of cells,

Humans, trees, and grass are all living things that grow and respond to their environments. The soil that sustains the plants is nonliving.

Cellular structure: All living things are composed of one or more cells that have a boundary called a membrane. This membrane not only separates the cell's interior from the environment but also encloses its genetic material in the form of DNA.

Responsiveness: Living organisms have the ability to detect changes in the environment and respond to them. This can include changes in the amount of light, heat, pressure, or chemicals in the surroundings. In most organisms, responsiveness also includes an ability to move, either to capture food or avoid damage.

Metabolism: Life-forms exist through their ability to take in and process chemical nutrients from the environment. Metabolism includes all internal chemical reactions by which organisms build molecules, obtain energy, and get rid of wastes.

Homeostasis: Because of the activity within their cells, living things are able to maintain their internal organization and processes at relatively constant conditions. This steady condition, or homeostasis, requires structures and functions that make adjustments for an ever-changing environment.

Growth, development, reproduction: All life-forms grow and change over time. Reproduction refers not only to producing new generations in the form of offspring but also to the cell division that allows multicellular organisms to increase in cell number.

Death: Everything that is alive will, at some point, cease to exist. Although individual life-forms die, reproduction ensures that a species will continue.

including the membrane, which is a film that keeps a cell intact and separates it from the outside environment. Cells are full of smaller structures, known as organelles (little organs). Each organelle plays a role in keeping the cell working properly. The cell has a nucleus, ribosomes, and other parts known

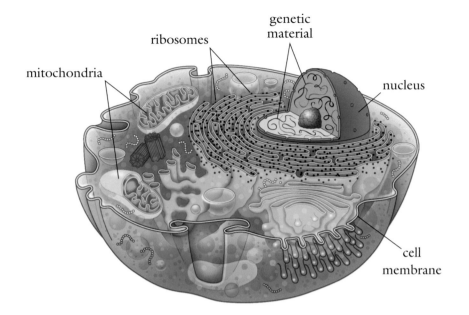

mitochondria

ribosomes

genetic
material

nucleus

cell
membrane

In addition to a membrane, complex cells contain a variety of smaller working parts known as organelles. The nucleus houses genetic material and directs cell activities. Ribosomes are protein factories, since a great amount of living tissue is made of protein. Mitochondria use sugars and oxygen to produce the energy needed to carry out cell functions, such as movement or building molecules. Other organelles contribute to such tasks as packaging cell products to send throughout the body or holding enzymes for cellular digestion.

as mitochondria. All of this cellular machinery is made up of chemicals that come from the food and air an organism takes in throughout its lifetime. Cells need nutrients and oxygen to generate energy for their functions. In a sense, we eat and breathe to give our cells structure and life.

Cells divide to form new cells. Once formed, the cell obtains nutrients, grows, gets rid of wastes, and makes products for its own use or for use by other cells in a complex body. When a cell gets to a certain size and age, it may divide into two new cells or it may die. A cell can die from a lack of nutrients, competition for space, poisons in its environment, battles with other cells, the malfunction of its organelles, or simply because it has worn out.

Some living things, such as bacteria, spend their entire life as a single cell. More complex organisms are made of many cells linked together. In the bodies of multicellular animals, such as humans, groups of living cells form sheets and layers known as tissues. Humans and many close animal relatives share the same types of tissues, including muscle, fat, and blood. Body organs are made up of collections of tissues. The heart, muscles, liver, brain, skin, and lungs are all organs. Some of these organs work closely with one another to form systems. For example, the digestive system is a collection of organs that work together. So is the respiratory system. All systems cooperate in a healthy, living body. Each has a role in maintaining life.

Maintaining a Healthy Balance

The proper coordination of body processes is a balancing act known as homeostasis. This term refers to keeping body conditions in an organism at a normal level. In humans this includes maintaining a normal body temperature, the proper blood sugar level, and a normal blood pressure. Homeostasis is a living body's ability to hold these conditions relatively constant.

A healthy human body has the amazing ability to maintain homeostasis without the person giving it a single thought. For example, despite the weather conditions outside, a body is able to keep a nearly constant internal temperature. If the outside temperature is very hot, the body will sweat. If it is cold, the body's metabolism and muscle activities keep it warm.

Many body conditions must be controlled very precisely for good health. Keeping body processes in balance requires the coordination of several different pathways and organs. In this example, increased blood pressure stretches vessel walls. A monitoring area in the brain senses this and responds by sending signals to the heart to slow down and reduce the force pushing blood through the circulatory system. This brings blood pressure back to normal.

Blood Pressure Maintained by a Feedback Cycle

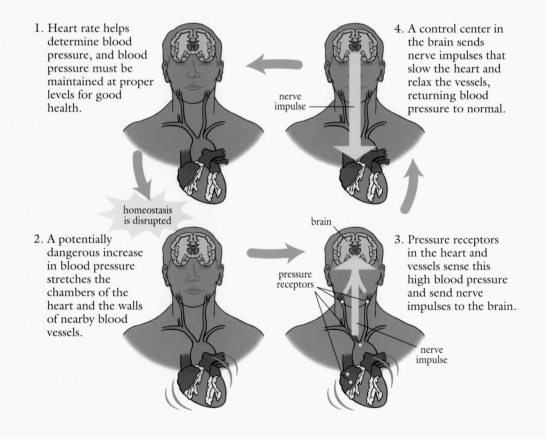

1. Heart rate helps determine blood pressure, and blood pressure must be maintained at proper levels for good health.

homeostasis is disrupted

2. A potentially dangerous increase in blood pressure stretches the chambers of the heart and the walls of nearby blood vessels.

nerve impulse

brain

pressure receptors

nerve impulse

3. Pressure receptors in the heart and vessels sense this high blood pressure and send nerve impulses to the brain.

4. A control center in the brain sends nerve impulses that slow the heart and relax the vessels, returning blood pressure to normal.

No matter what a person eats, a healthy person's blood sugar will not become dangerously high. The hormone insulin adjusts it to normal. Between meals, body processes tap into the reserves of energy stored in cells to keep functioning. The body constantly adjusts respiration rate and blood pressure to make sure each and every organ is getting its share of oxygen and nutrients. These balancing acts go on all day, every day, in a body whose systems, organs, tissues, cells, and cellular organelles are normal.

All the parts of the body are linked in some way to one another, and each is responsible for helping maintain homeostasis. We breathe and eat to keep our cells working and full of energy. Our cells keep us alive so we can keep breathing and eating. Because the parts of the body rely on one another, a failure in one structure or function can have an effect on the whole organism. Extreme failures on any level can be catastrophic. In this way, life, health, disease, and death are all tied together.

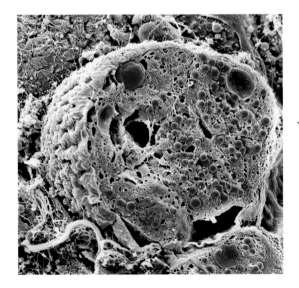

This image shows a magnified pancreas cell. The pancreas is an organ that produces chemicals that help to regulate blood sugar and assist digestion.

MAJOR HUMAN BODY SYSTEMS

Cardiovascular system: The blood, heart, and blood vessels work together to transport nutrients, oxygen, hormones, heat, and cellular wastes. Some blood cells are important in defense against foreign invaders.

Digestive system: The digestive system breaks down food and absorbs the nutrients in it. This system consists of a tube that runs from the mouth and stomach to the anus, as well as the liver, gallbladder, and pancreas.

Endocrine system: Many glands of the body, including the pancreas, thyroid, and adrenal glands, produce chemical hormones that travel through the blood to help direct cell and organ activities.

Integumentary system: Composed of the skin and its glands, hair, and nails, this system forms a protective, waterproof barrier to the outside world.

Lymphatic system: Lymph vessels collect excess fluid from tissues and return it to the bloodstream. Lymphatic organs such as the spleen, tonsils, and lymph nodes protect against bacteria and viruses.

Muscular system: Most muscles attach to bones. They contract to produce movement. Muscle activity creates much of our body heat.

Nervous system: Consisting of the brain, spinal cord, and nerves that extend off them, the nervous system communicates with the rest of the body through electrical signals and controls many body activities.

Reproductive system: Different in males and females, this system produces sex cells known as sperm and eggs that can combine to form offspring. The female body is adapted to nourish her developing child.

Respiratory system: The airways extending from the nose and mouth carry air to and from the lungs. Blood absorbs oxygen from the air we breathe, and toxic carbon dioxide leaves the body through these airways.

Skeletal system: Made of bones and joints, the skeleton functions in support and protection of other body structures. Bone is the body's mineral warehouse, and bone marrow forms blood cells.

Urinary system: The kidneys work constantly to filter the blood, removing harmful waste products and excess water. These are passed to the bladder, where they are held until excreted as urine.

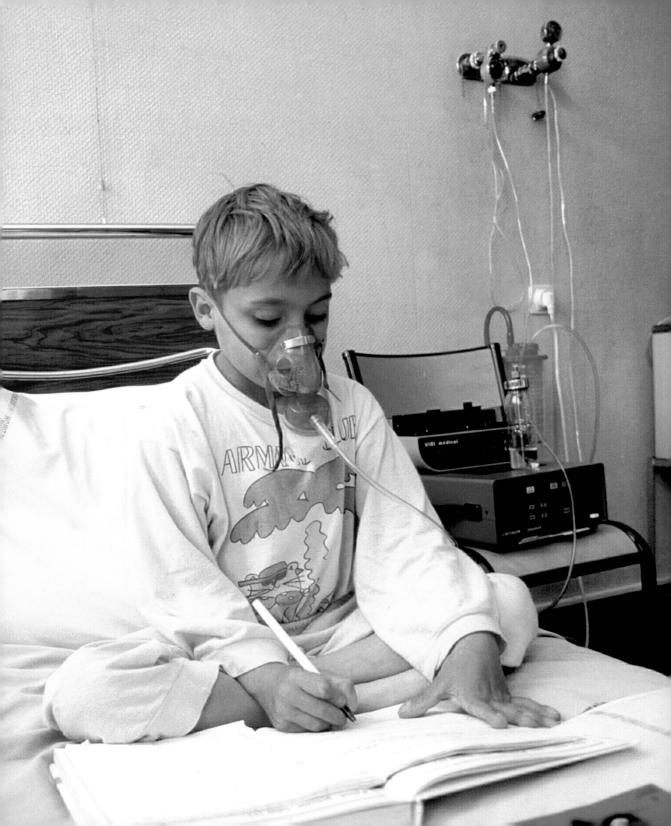

Chapter 2

THE BODY IN CRISIS

When the body malfunctions, the result is known as a disorder or disease. A disease can be caused by anything that stresses the body to a point where homeostasis cannot be easily restored. We usually think of stress as a state of mind, such as being stressed out because of an important test in school or a serious family problem. But in scientific terms, stress is anything that disturbs homeostasis. This includes very cold or hot temperatures, harmful bacteria or viruses that break through body defenses, dehydration (loss of body fluids), loss of blood, lack of oxygen, or anything else that can damage cells. The mind can also experience disease-causing stress. Because the brain is an organ that controls other organs and all body systems are linked, people can worry themselves sick if they suffer from tremendous mental stress.

Scientists classify certain negative changes in the body's structures and functions as a particular disease. Strep throat, Alzheimer's disease, the common cold, heart disease, cystic fibrosis, asthma, cancer, stomach ulcers, stroke, and even sunburn are a few of the many forms of disorder or disease. Obviously, some disorders are mild. Others are far more serious.

A boy does his homework in a hospital while undergoing treatment for cystic fibrosis. Cystic fibrosis is a disorder of cell membranes that causes imbalances in body fluids. This disease results in severe problems in breathing and digestion. Medical treatments can help people with cystic fibrosis, but the disorder usually causes an early death.

DEFENDING THE BODY AGAINST HARM

Skin: The intact skin is the body's first line of defense against bacteria, viruses, chemicals, sunlight, and general wear and tear. It is composed of many layers of tightly packed cells that contain a waterproof protein to help us retain body fluids. These skin cells also hold variable amounts of pigment to shield us from excessive sun. Because the skin cells on the top layer are dead, they are regularly shed and replaced. Although the top layer carries a tremendous number of bacteria, the constant loss of surface cells helps keep skin bacteria under control.

Mucous membranes: Mucous membranes line body passages that are open to the environment. This includes much of the respiratory, digestive, urinary, and reproductive systems. Mucus is a thick secretion that traps microorganisms and other foreign substances, such as dust in the respiratory tract. Some internal surfaces have tiny hairlike projections to sweep mucous membranes of debris. Like the skin, the surface cells of mucous membranes are shed to control bacteria. Coughing and sneezing also help remove invaders.

Liquid defenses: Other fluids also wash body surfaces. Tears flow across the eyes as we blink, perspiration pushes away bacteria, and the oil in our skin helps make a protective barrier. Swallowing saliva takes bacteria in our mouth to our stomach where acids can destroy them. Vomiting and diarrhea are means of expelling toxins or pathogens (germs) that reach harmful levels in our digestive tract. The flow of urine regularly flushes away most bacteria in our urinary tract. Many of the body's surface fluids also contain chemicals that defend us from invasion.

Cellular defenses: When pathogens break through our intact skin or mucous membranes, internal cellular defenses take over. Our blood has white cells that destroy invaders and abnormal cells. When tissue is damaged, blood vessels in the injured area open more fully to allow increased blood flow. This inflammatory response includes redness, swelling, pain, and heat. A fever is the body's way of creating a hostile temperature environment for bacteria.

Some medical problems come on rather suddenly. They are known as acute diseases. Other disorders recur often or last for long periods. They are called chronic diseases. A mild disorder is one that the body usually takes care of reasonably well, either by itself or with minor medical treatment. These include strep throat, a cold, or sunburn. Diseases are serious when the body's homeostasis regulators cannot correct the problem over time. In these cases, drastic medical treatment is necessary. Sometimes even the best medical practices cannot cure a disease, and the result is death. Other causes of death are unrelated to disease. They result from trauma to the body. A serious car accident, drowning, suffocation, or a gunshot wound can cause the death of an otherwise healthy person.

We often associate some diseases with a particular body system or organ, such as heart disease. An unhealthy heart has difficulty pumping oxygen and nutrients to the rest of the body cells, so they suffer too. A respiratory system problem such as asthma or cystic fibrosis can limit the ability of the lungs to get

Blocked arteries, such as this one, lead to heart disease. When blood cannot flow properly, tissues do not get the nutrients they need.

enough air. Then all tissue cells will experience a lack of oxygen. Diseases aren't restricted to the system and organ level, though. Many diseases happen on the cellular level, yet they affect the entire body.

Top Causes of Death in the United States in 2006

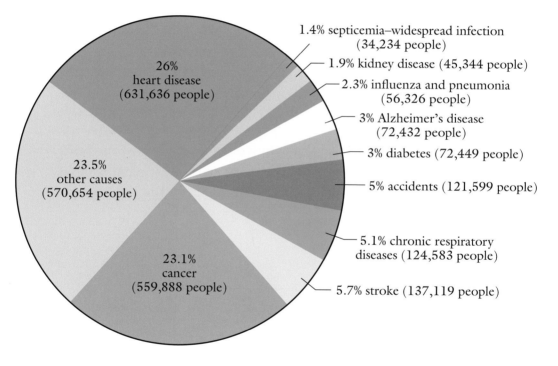

26%
heart disease
(631,636 people)

1.4% septicemia–widespread infection
(34,234 people)

1.9% kidney disease (45,344 people)

2.3% influenza and pneumonia
(56,326 people)

3% Alzheimer's disease
(72,432 people)

3% diabetes (72,449 people)

5% accidents (121,599 people)

5.1% chronic respiratory
diseases (124,583 people)

5.7% stroke (137,119 people)

23.5%
other causes
(570,654 people)

23.1%
cancer
(559,888 people)

Total number of deaths in the United States in 2006: 2,426,264

Trauma is the leading cause of death in the United States for people younger than forty-four years old.

SEARCHING OUT DEADLY CELLS

Carl L. Parrott, MD, pathologist

As a pathologist, it is my responsibility to search for the origins of disease and injury and to study their effects on cells, tissues, and organs. In order to recognize what is abnormal, I need to have a deep understanding of all levels of normal anatomy and physiology. Today genetic tests and molecular analyses are becoming more common, but the microscope still remains the primary tool used by a pathologist when searching for disease. This is because the clues to distinguish one disorder from another reveal themselves through microscopic changes in the appearance of cells and tissues.

Typically, before a pathologist identifies a disease, another physician first detects a problem in a patient, perhaps using an X-ray or some other test, or simply through a physical examination. Next, a sample of suspicious tissue is removed from the patient and submitted to a pathologist for examination. Under the microscope, cells and tissues may exhibit inflammation, which may be a sign of infection. Abnormal or excessive cell growth could indicate cancer. Although traumatic injuries affect whole organs or even the entire body, most human diseases occur at the level of tissues and their cells.

The pathologist's role in health care is to identify specific disorders so the appropriate treatment can be decided upon and started. Our input can benefit not only the individual patient, but also the patient's family and community, and contribute to the scientific understanding of disease.

Delving Deeper into Disease

The chronic condition of high blood sugar, known as diabetes, affects many body systems. But it usually results from cells in the organ called the pancreas not working properly. These cells in the pancreas produce the hormone insulin. Insulin keeps blood sugar within homeostatic ranges by helping that sugar enter cells, where it can be used to make energy. If cells of the pancreas fail to manufacture enough insulin, cells throughout the body suffer. In diabetes the lack of insulin prevents cells from taking in and using the sugar in the blood. This causes abnormally high levels of sugar in the blood, while cells starve and malfunction.

Sickle cell anemia is a genetic disease in which a defective gene causes red blood cells to have an abnormal shape. Red blood cells carry oxygen through the bloodstream. The malformed blood cells caused by sickle cell anemia have trouble carrying oxygen. They also have difficulty moving smoothly through blood vessels. Because the bloodstream is the lifeline of the entire body, all tissues can suffer from lack of oxygen and poor circulation as a result of sickle cell anemia.

Cystic fibrosis is a genetic disorder of cell membranes. People with cystic fibrosis have cells that fail to maintain the proper balance of chemicals outside and inside of them. This causes problems with the balance of fluid in the body's tissues. As a result, thick mucus forms in many body passages. The mucus blocks the release of some enzymes (chemicals needed to break down food in the digestive tract). This results in malnutrition. The most serious problems with cystic fibrosis, however, occur when thick fluid collects in airways and lungs. The fluids block the respiratory tract and limit the amount of air the lungs can hold. This means lower oxygen levels in all

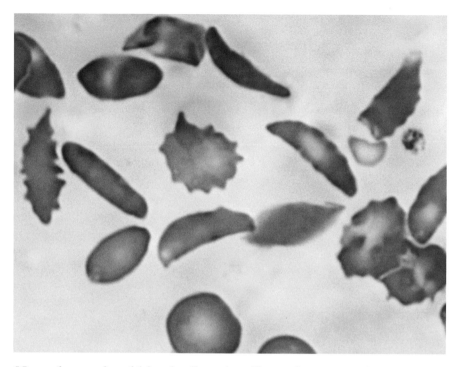

Normal, round, red blood cells and malformed, crescent-shaped cells appear in the bloodstream of a person suffering from sickle cell anemia.

body tissues. These thickened fluids in the lungs also allow infections to thrive. Because of the many severe problems cystic fibrosis can cause, it is a terminal condition. This means that the disease is likely to take the patient's life by one complication or another.

These examples illustrate how body systems rely on one another and on properly functioning cells to maintain life. They also show that cells need body organs to work correctly to deliver the chemicals cells need to do their jobs. These diseases often lead to death because of the wide-ranging effects they have on all body systems.

LIVING WITH A TERMINAL DISEASE

Jamie Murray, cystic fibrosis patient

Because I have a serious and life-threatening illness, I believe both my daily life and long-term goals are significantly different than those of my friends. I have to do a lot of extra work to stay as healthy as possible.

I wake up an hour early each day to inhale a variety of medications and use a vest device that shakes my lungs. Because I also have to do this at night (and more often if I am sick), it complicates hanging out with my friends. Travel is difficult because I have to lug around machines. I also have to take a variety of medications with my food. Having CF causes me to get sick more than the average person, and I have already had about twenty-five surgeries. All of that means missing a lot of school.

I am constantly faced with a life or death situation in the very act of taking care of myself each day. Because of this, I believe I have become a deeper thinker than most people my age. In college, I am a philosophy major and someday would like to help other people with chronic illnesses take control of their lives and make it through the tough times.

Disease, Disability, and Death

When a person dies, whether from injury or disease, the basic cause of death is that a certain number of that person's cells stopped working. If enough cells in a tissue die, that tissue ceases to function. If the tissues making up an organ no longer work, that organ can fail. The failure of one organ impairs the body system to which it belongs. And since systems are connected to one another, the entire body can shut down. So if enough cells in the body die—or certain types of cells in the body die—the entire organism may die.

Consider a heart attack. It is often caused by chemicals, such as fats and cholesterol, that build up in blood vessels. The heart is an organ composed mostly of muscle tissue. Like other muscles of the body, the heart has blood vessels that feed its cells with the oxygen and nutrients needed to create energy. This energy powers the contractions of the heart. These contractions pump blood through the arteries and create the pressure that pushes blood to all tissues of the body. When a blood vessel leading to the heart becomes clogged, cells of the heart will starve and die. This is a heart attack. If enough heart cells die, there may not be enough healthy muscle in the wall of the heart to push blood through the circulatory system.

Whether someone survives a heart attack often depends on how many cells in the heart die and where those cells are. If a large number of heart muscle cells die in a spot that is critical to the flow of blood, the damage may be so severe that the heart will stop beating. When this happens, the flow of blood through the entire body stops. Then necessary nutrients and oxygen will not reach the rest of the cells, tissues, and organs. As a result of heart failure, cells in distant organs will also shut down. Multiple organs and systems will stop working. Death will be the likely outcome.

People who survive heart attacks do so because fewer heart muscle cells die. Depending on the amount of damage, these heart attack survivors may have lifelong problems delivering oxygen and nutrients to tissues. This will cause weakness in muscles and other organs. Another heart attack can lead to further damage or death.

Strokes also illustrate how the effects of a disease depend on how many and which cells of an organ are affected. A stroke is a form of brain damage. It results when blood flow to brain cells is interrupted. A stroke can be the result of a blocked blood vessel, similar to what happens to the heart during a heart attack. A stroke can also occur when a brain blood vessel ruptures, or bursts, sending the blood into places it does not belong.

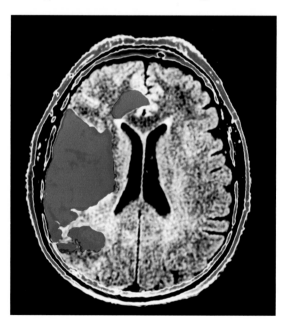

This computer scan shows the brain of a person who suffered a stroke. The red areas show the places where blood has escaped into the brain. Strokes can cause serious brain damage and death.

LIVING THROUGH HEART ATTACKS AND STROKE

Charles Raiford Jr., survivor

As a younger man, I spent nine years in the Coast Guard, and even on-board a ship, I had a pretty decent diet and medical care. After that, I didn't think much about my eating habits or my health, plus I smoked.

About ten years ago, a voice inside told me to get a physical, because I hadn't had one since the service. I was diabetic and didn't even know. The doctors told me to go on a strict diet and stop smoking, but I eventually reverted to old habits. Four years later, while walking to work, I had my first heart attack. I was treated for that and got better, but I still smoked a little—I was pretty hard-headed. Just last year, I had another heart attack, and again, my symptoms led me to the emergency room for treatment.

A few months later, I had a stroke. Luckily, at the time, I worked at a hospital and was treated immediately. If I had been at home, I probably would have died. With the stroke, there was no warning and no symptoms, and this time I was really afraid I was going to die. Even after months of treatment, my whole left side is weak, and I am in a wheelchair but am learning to use a cane. I am blessed, though, that I didn't lose my thinking ability. Here's how I am thinking now: I have a lot of regrets about not taking better care of myself. I am done being selfish and I am going to work hard to get back to one hundred percent. I have two boys and I want to see them grow up. I want to be here for them.

If a brain vessel ruptures, brain cells beyond that point don't receive their normal flow of blood. How much a patient is disabled by a stroke depends on how many and which brain cells die from a lack of oxygen and nutrients. The brain is responsible for speech, movement, sensation, and many other body processes. A person will lose the functions controlled by the specific brain regions that die. If the stroke affects the reflex centers of the brain, which control heart rate, blood pressure, or breathing, the result may be death.

Those who survive a heart attack are living with some dead heart muscle cells. People who have had strokes live with areas of dead tissue in their brains. As with heart attack survivors, there is always the risk that a stroke victim who suffers another stroke will be further impaired or may die.

Heart attacks and strokes are only two examples of disorders that can destroy cells, tissues, organs, or systems. Think of all the body systems, the organs each contains, and the chemical reactions going on inside cells to keep us alive. Then imagine how many problems can arise at each level of these functions. We know that death is inevitable, but because of the complexity of the body and the world in which we live, there are countless ways that a life can end.

Can It Be Fixed?

When extreme conditions or invaders cause more stress than the body can withstand, disease or death occurs. Problems may begin inside the body or they may develop from outside it, but the result is the same. Cells and tissues are harmed. Internal failures include high blood pressure that blows out a vessel and causes a stroke or cancer cells that starve normal tissue cells.

Outside causes of damage include infection from bacteria or blood loss from a serious wound.

Ultimately, however, external agents are harmful because they cause internal failures. For instance, an accidental fall may involve a severe blow to the head. This could cause the rupture of vessels and bleeding within the skull. This bleeding interrupts the normal flow of blood to cells in the brain, and those cells die.

In another case, a poisonous snake's bite to the leg sends toxins into the bloodstream. The toxins can destroy oxygen-carrying red blood cells or cause nerve cells to malfunction or die. When nerve cells malfunction, the brain can't receive information from or send instructions to muscles and other important organs. If nerve cells that carry messages to the muscles of breathing are damaged, death will result from failure of the respiratory system. These internal failures in organs, tissues, and cells are what lead to disorder or death, regardless of the external source of the damage to the body.

The body's ability to restore normal structure and function depends on the extent of the injury or disease. A seriously bleeding wound, for example, cannot be healed by the same blood clotting ability that heals a paper cut. No amount of clotting can seal off a large opening that has drastically punctured the body's defenses. Even if someone is able to compress or tie off an injury such as this, it still may be too little or too late. When too much blood is lost, the body cannot maintain blood pressure at a level that will deliver nutrients to tissue cells. Organ failure may result. The heart may speed up in an attempt to increase pressure, but without enough blood in the body, a frantic heartbeat is just not enough.

Time is also a factor in an injury such as a poisonous snakebite. Once the toxins have entered the victim, the pumping action of the heart will deliver the poison in the blood to other parts of the body over time. The person might be rushed to the hospital and receive an antidote to the toxin. But if too much time has elapsed, the toxin can cause a great deal of tissue damage. Death or serious disability—such as the loss of the limb that was bitten—can be the result.

The outcome of any disorder or injury depends on a number of things. These include the body parts damaged, the seriousness of the problem, and how quickly normal function can or cannot be restored. A drowning victim, for example, may be revived if removed from the water and treated quickly. First aid, including cardiopulmonary resuscitation (CPR), may restart the heartbeat and restore breathing and oxygen circulation. Still, if the person's brain lacked oxygen for about four minutes or longer, some brain cells will have died. As with a stroke, the number of brain cells affected and their location determine how serious the injury will be. The reflex centers that govern heart rate and breathing may resume their functions. This will keep the person's body alive. But if the higher centers of information processing have been severely damaged, the person may never regain consciousness or may be paralyzed for life.

In some cases of brain damage, a patient may remain in a coma or some type of altered state of consciousness indefinitely. This includes what is known as a vegetative state. This term is used when a patient appears aware but unresponsive, yet still retains the basic reflexes necessary to maintain life. In other cases of irreversible brain damage, even vital reflex centers will stop working. This can result in failure of the victim's heartbeat and breathing. Such a person is considered to be brain dead. High-tech devices may move a patient's blood to keep body cells supplied with oxygen and nutrients, but the victim lacks all brain function and cannot survive without the equipment that is providing circulation.

Some effects of stress or injury are reversible, and others are

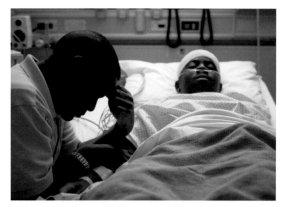

A person in a coma receives medical care. Sometimes while in a deep coma, the body heals and eventually consciousness returns.

not. Cells that die will not come back to life. But natural repairing processes can heal surprisingly serious damage to the body, especially with medical help. It all depends upon the severity of the injury, upon which organ is damaged, and often upon how quickly medical care can begin.

Recognizing an Emergency

When a life-threatening wound occurs, as in a car accident or by gunshot, rapid medical care is crucial. Paramedic and emergency room teams are trained to meet the needs of critically injured patients. They take swift action when the damage to tissues and organs goes beyond the body's own ability to repair them. Speedy treatment benefits the healing process even in situations that are not life threatening. For example, a broken bone will heal faster when the fracture can be quickly set.

In cases of chronic disease, a person must recognize when the symptoms are severe enough to seek medical help. Unfortunately, the signs of some diseases are not obvious. Cancer, for example, is a disorder of uncontrolled cell division. Cancerous cells divide rapidly and invade nearby tissues. They form a mass called a malignant tumor. This mass competes with normal cells for space and nutrients. A person's cardiovascular system pumps blood to these hungry and aggressive cancer cells, and the tumor grows. A person may only know to seek medical help when the tumor is large enough to be detected. By that time, the cancer cells may have already spread to other parts of the body, sometimes traveling in the bloodstream. Even if the original tumor is detected and treated, future tumors may already be forming elsewhere.

High blood pressure and other types of cardiovascular disease also may show few symptoms. Even a heart attack can be misleading. Patients may experience the pain in their shoulder, jaw, or arm. This is because the brain often has difficulty pinpointing the source of internal pain.

Medical help can save lives in many cases of acute injury or chronic disease. Urgent care can effectively treat life-threatening conditions, such as serious blood loss, a head injury, a heart attack, smoke inhalation, an overdose of drugs, or a severe electric shock. Treatment for long-term diseases—such as cancer, liver or gallbladder problems, diabetes, sickle cell anemia, cystic fibrosis, or a severe case of pneumonia—may be helped with long or frequent hospital stays.

Even with all the medical advances of modern times, however, lives are still lost. Some patients never make it to an emergency room or are too late. People with chronic diseases can have the best medical care, but finally the disease may lead to their death. All humans die of one disorder or another. Some die rather suddenly. Others linger with a long-term disability. Some people die young. Others live to be very old before their organs begin to fail. In the end, the fate of all living creatures is death. In that sense, life itself is a terminal condition.

WHEN A LIFE CANNOT BE SAVED

Michael Hayes, paramedic and firefighter

From a paramedic's standpoint, the treatment for a dying patient generally does not differ from the care given to any other patient. Since the role of a paramedic is to provide emergency care, we are obligated to follow specific treatment instructions and, in most circumstances, are not at liberty to diminish or alter patient care.

Scientific signs that a person is dying include falling blood pressure, changes in heart rate and electrical rhythm, respiratory changes, and altered mental state or loss of consciousness. These findings may also be present in sick or injured patients who are not dying. However, in a dying patient, system failure cannot be stabilized through treatment, and as a result, the patient's condition continues to deteriorate.

A paramedic may withhold care if a patient has sustained major trauma in which the injuries are incompatible with life, or there are obvious signs of death, such as rigor mortis or decomposition. Although laws vary, many states allow paramedics to discontinue care if they have provided appropriate treatment and resuscitation attempts were unsuccessful. Guidelines specify that the patient must not be breathing, have no pulse or cardiac electrical activity, and everyone involved must be in agreement in discontinuing care. This includes the paramedics and the medical control physician with whom they are consulting during the emergency run.

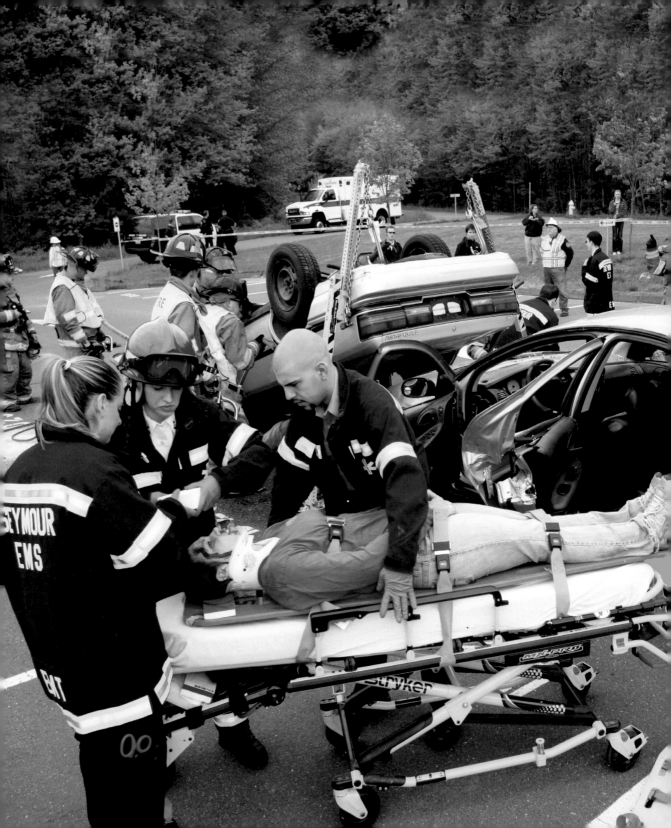

Chapter 3

DEATH'S TIMETABLE

Whether gradual or sudden, death is actually a series of events that occurs over time. In the case of gradual illness, the timeline is drawn out over weeks, months, or maybe even years. Typically, as a chronic disease advances, more and more cells malfunction or die. This leads to tissues and organs that are less able to carry out their functions. One by one, organs fail until one or more systems simply shut down. Although some organs can be replaced through organ transplants, a chronic illness eventually ruins enough tissue to lead to death.

Even a seemingly quick death is really a series of events over a brief period of time. The timeline of death can be minutes or longer. Heart function and respiration may slow dramatically. They may even stop and restart several times during the actual dying process. Death can happen in a matter of seconds in an explosion, a fall from a great height, or other serious accidents. Typically, however, what appears to be the moment of death is really the result of processes that have been going on over several minutes or hours.

During the normal course of aging, cells and their functions break down. At the same time, the body's ability to repair damaged cells or replace dead cells decreases. In that sense, once we mature to adulthood, we are all slowly dying. Some tissues, such as the skin and blood, have an amazing ability to renew

Emergency workers demonstrate rescue techniques at a mock car crash. Every second counts after an accident, because the dying process may start well before help arrives.

themselves throughout a lifetime. Cells deep within the skin constantly divide. These are one type of stem cell. These stem cells form new skin cells that are pushed to the body's surface. During this journey, they die and then flake off. The total life span of a typical skin cell, from its formation to its death, is about four weeks. In a similar way, stem cells in bone marrow produce new red blood cells—usually at an amazing rate of about two million

THE IMPORTANCE OF STEM CELLS

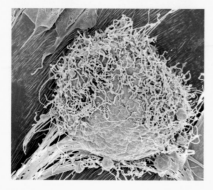

Stem cells are immature cells that have yet to take on a specific role within the body. They are present in large numbers within the growing embryo. Stem cells in an embryo are still capable of forming any tissue in the body. Humans retain some stem cells throughout life. The skin houses stem cells capable of forming new skin. Bone marrow has stem cells *(left)* that continually renew blood cells.

Stem cells have the potential to cure some diseases by using them to replace cells that have faulty genes or cells that have stopped functioning properly. Scientists can work with stem cells from embryos to advance research in this field. Human bone marrow stem cell transplants can already remedy some blood diseases.

Some people object to stem cell research because they oppose using embryos for scientific purposes. Stem cell therapy can also impose new risks to a patient, since using stem cell treatment involves shutting down the immune system of the recipient. This decreases their protection against other diseases. As research in the field progresses and if society can embrace the benefits of stem cell therapy, it may be an important part of medical treatment in the future.

Lifting weights can increase muscle size, but it does not create new cells. Instead, it makes the muscle cells bigger.

per second. The reason for this constant production is that red blood cells only live for about four months in circulation. Mature red blood cells aren't able to divide, and moving through the narrowest of blood vessels wears them out. The body's ability to create new skin and blood cells from stem cells decreases over time, however. So the skin has a harder time healing as people age.

Some tissues do not replace their cells well or at all. Once they are mature, muscle cells cannot divide. They can only enlarge by adding more proteins within their cell membranes. Even bodybuilders who add great mass to their muscles are not creating new cells. They are simply pumping up the cells they already have. In addition, although the brain grows dramatically during the first few years of life, by early childhood, humans have all the nerve cells they will ever have. After that, nerve cells simply get larger and change, depending on a person's experiences. Damage to the nervous system, particularly to the brain and spinal cord, can be only partly repaired, if at all.

Physical therapists work with a man recovering from a spinal cord injury. Most damage to the brain and spinal cord is permanent, although some functions can be regained through treatment.

Every single cell in an organism's body has a life and death of its own. Because tissues are made of cells and organs are composed of tissues, tissues and organs have a life span too. The healing process is one of the ways our body and its cells try to restore homeostasis after disease or injury. But as people age, muscles lose their strength, bones may weaken, reflexes slow down, senses may begin to fail, and repair mechanisms decline. The ability to generate new cells and repair or replace damaged ones varies with age and the tissue involved. Some tissue cells are programmed to die and be replaced often. Others are meant to last a lifetime.

REPAIRING AND REPLACING DAMAGED TISSUES

Surface tissues: Skin and mucous membranes constantly renew their surface by the division of stem cells that reside in deeper layers. For this reason, when these tissues are damaged, they tend to heal rapidly and well. Superficial injuries often leave no scar because these surfaces are designed to withstand wear and tear.

Support tissues: Supportive tissues in the body have different powers of healing and regeneration. Blood cells are replaced constantly by cell division. Although the number of fat-storage cells in the adult is limited, these cells can hold increasing amounts of fat. The number of fat cells remains the same even when weight is gained or lost. Bone usually heals well, due to a rich blood supply that carries the ingredients to manufacture new bone. Cartilage has a very poor blood supply and heals much more slowly.

Muscle tissue: Voluntary muscle tissue, such as in the muscles that move our bones, loses the ability to divide and replace lost cells after birth. These muscles have only limited ability to repair themselves. Muscle in the heart typically dies after a heart attack, but recent evidence suggests some repair and even cell replacement is possible. Other involuntary muscles, such as in the walls of hollow organs like the uterus and blood vessels, retain some stem cells and have much better regeneration than other muscle types.

Nervous tissue: After birth, very few information-processing stem cells remain in the brain. Even in the first few years of life, growth of the brain and spinal cord is mostly due to an increase in the size of these cells, not their number. For this reason, damage to the brain or spinal cord is usually permanent. Some nerves that connect to the brain or spinal cord can heal if injured (such as those in the hands and feet), but repair can take time or may not occur at all.

How Long Is a Lifetime?

Before antibiotics were developed, even the smallest wounds could cause serious bacterial infections that resulted in death. When antidotes for poisons were not known, toxins that entered the body were often fatal. Attempts at surgery were often deadly before disease-causing germs and the workings of the body were well understood.

Scientists estimate that the average life expectancy of Stone Age people was about eighteen to thirty-three years. Life spans have increased throughout history, and the worldwide average is now about sixty-six years.

LIFE EXPECTANCY

It is estimated that prehistoric humans (Paleolithic, Neolithic, and Bronze Age) had average life spans between eighteen and forty years, depending on the region of the world and specific period of time. Classic Greeks and Romans, as well as Medieval British people, had an average life expectancy of between twenty and thirty years. Before the arrival of Europeans, Native Americans lived on average twenty-five to thirty-five years.

In the United States, the life span averaged forty-seven years in 1900, sixty-eight years in 1950, and seventy-seven years in 2000. The current worldwide average life expectancy is about sixty-six years but varies greatly by country. Women tend to live longer than men. Throughout recorded history, life span has been related to status in society, access to health care, and periods when infectious diseases ravaged parts of the world. The current AIDS epidemic in Africa is responsible for the lowest worldwide life expectancies seen there today.

LIFE EXPECTANCIES AT BIRTH FOR SELECTED COUNTRIES

Over 80 years — Australia, Canada, France, Japan, Sweden, Switzerland (Japan is highest at 82.07 years)

75–80 years — Argentina, Austria, Belgium, Chile, Cuba, Czech Republic, Denmark, Ecuador, Finland, Germany, Greece, Israel, Italy, Jordan, Libya, Mexico, Netherlands, Paraguay, Poland, Portugal, Saudi Arabia, Serbia, South Korea, Spain, Taiwan, Tunisia, United Kingdom, United States (78.06 years)

70–75 years — Algeria, Belarus, Brazil, Bulgaria, Columbia, Dominican Republic, Egypt, El Salvador, Hungary, Indonesia, Iran, Malaysia, Morocco, Nicaragua, North Korea, People's Republic of China, Peru, Philippines, Romania, Slovakia, Sri Lanka, Syria, Thailand, Turkey, Venezuela, Vietnam

65–70 years — Azerbaijan, Bolivia, Guatemala, Honduras, India, Iraq, Kazakhstan, Kyrgyzstan, Papua New Guinea, Russia, Turkmenistan, Ukraine

60–65 years — Bangladesh, Cambodia, Madagascar, Myanmar, Nepal, Pakistan, Tajikistan, Uzbekistan, Yemen

55–60 years — Democratic Republic of the Congo, Eritrea, Ghana, Haiti, Kenya, Laos, Senegal, Togo

50–55 years — Benin, Burundi, Cameroon, Tanzania, Uganda

Under 50 years — Afghanistan, Angola, Burkina Faso, Chad, Côte d'Ivoire, Ethiopia, Guinea, Malawi, Mali, Mozambique, Niger, Nigeria, Rwanda, Sierra Leone, Somalia, South Africa, Sudan, Zambia, Zimbabwe (Angola is lowest at 37.63 years)

(2008 CIA *World Factbook*)

People are living longer not only because of advances in medical care but also because of improved nutrition during the early and mid 1900s. The modern epidemic of childhood obesity and poor nutrition from junk food in the United States may affect the life span of today's young people in the years to come. Clearly, a relationship exists between general health and nutrition and how long people live.

Nutrition and access to medical care are not the same around the world, however. What qualifies as old age may depend on where a person lives. Whether someone dies from an infection or has a chance for an organ transplant may depend more on his or her country or income than on age. People around the world have different disease threats and life stresses. People with a poor diet or those exposed to harsh living conditions often seem to grow old faster than others.

Even in the absence of disease, some elderly people reach an age when their bodies simply give out. We might say they died of old age. Our cells, tissues, organs, and systems are just not programmed to last forever.

Death Is Inevitable, but Is It Expected?

A doctor can often identify an illness and discuss its prognosis with the patient. The term *prognosis* refers to the projected outcome or most likely course that a disease will take. A patient's prognosis may depend on whether he or she seeks treatment. For example, a cancer patient may be told he or she is projected to live six months without treatment. The patient could live longer by undergoing treatments such as surgery, chemotherapy, or radiation therapy. Each patient's prognosis and course of treatment depends on the type of cancer and how soon it is detected.

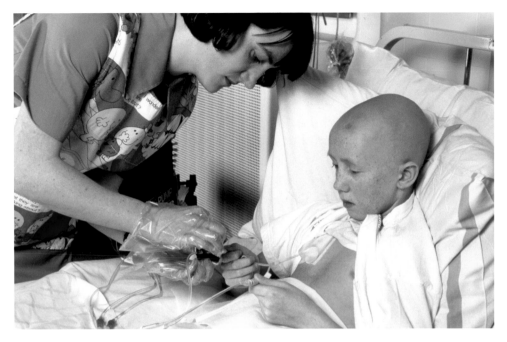

A nurse administers chemotherapy drugs to a boy with leukemia. Leukemia is a cancer of the blood that results from the faulty production of white blood cells.

Many forms of treatment have side effects that stress the body. But patients accept them if the benefits are thought to outweigh the risks. Chemotherapy drugs are toxic substances that target rapidly dividing cells. They attack the cells within a cancer tumor, which are constantly dividing as they form a mass. As a side effect of chemotherapy, other cell types that rapidly divide during normal tissue growth and replacement are also damaged. These include hair cells, skin cells, and blood cells. If the cancer treatment is successful, the body usually heals after the cancer is defeated. Many cancer survivors go on to live long and healthy lives.

Many other chronic diseases have a fairly predictable outcome. People born with genetic diseases such as sickle cell anemia or cystic fibrosis undergo treatments throughout their entire life. Other long-term conditions, such as osteoarthritis, may be related to the natural aging of joints and related tissues. They are not life-threatening disorders and may require treatment only in old age. Some chronic illnesses are known to cause increasing disability as they progress over a patient's lifetime. They are often directly responsible for the person's death. These include illnesses such as emphysema and chronic bronchitis that result in steady declines in lung function. Many cardiovascular (heart and circulation) diseases typically worsen over time and are finally fatal. Life habits such as smoking, not getting enough exercise, or a poor diet can cause chronic disease states that ultimately lead to death.

Other long-term conditions may cause a person's death more indirectly. This is the case with Alzheimer's disease and Lou Gehrig's disease (also known as amyotrophic lateral sclerosis, or ALS), which affect parts of the nervous system. In these disorders, the patient gradually loses control of body functions, often including the ability to move and breathe properly. As the person becomes more disabled and less active, fluids collect in the lungs, and bacteria can easily breed there. This leads to respiratory infections, such as pneumonia. These infections—not the chronic illness—become the actual direct cause of death.

Acquired immunodeficiency syndrome, known as AIDS, is also a chronic disease that leads to other infections. In AIDS the immune system is weakened so much that another disorder, such as cancer or pneumonia, can easily move in and lead to death. Unlike some other chronic diseases, though, a person of any age can contract AIDS. It is an infectious disorder that is transmitted from person to person, regardless of the victim's age.

An allergy is another chronic condition that may not relate to a person's age. Many allergies, such as to plant pollen or to pet dander, are generally not severe. Serious allergies, however, can cause severe respiratory problems. The airways can swell closed, causing suffocation. A person with a serious allergy to peanuts or a bee sting, for example, must know he or she has that allergy to avoid its cause.

What about those people who suddenly drop dead without any known cause? In some cases of unexpected death, the victim, the family, and his or her physician did not know of any serious disorder or condition. A seemingly healthy young athlete may die of no apparent reason on the basketball court. Only later, through an autopsy, the pathologist may discover that the victim had a faulty heart valve that had never been discovered. The person's heart had adapted to this chronic condition over the years. Without showing any outward signs, this athlete's body changed the way his heart functioned. It maintained homeostasis despite the faulty valve. Eventually, however, when stressed beyond its limited ability, the malformed heart gave out.

When a death is the result of a naturally occurring disease process, whether expected or not, officials use the term *natural causes*. Death from natural causes often follows a predictable course of symptoms and stages. Scientists have studied the body changes that signal the coming of death. Health-care professionals can track its progress in a patient known to be close to dying.

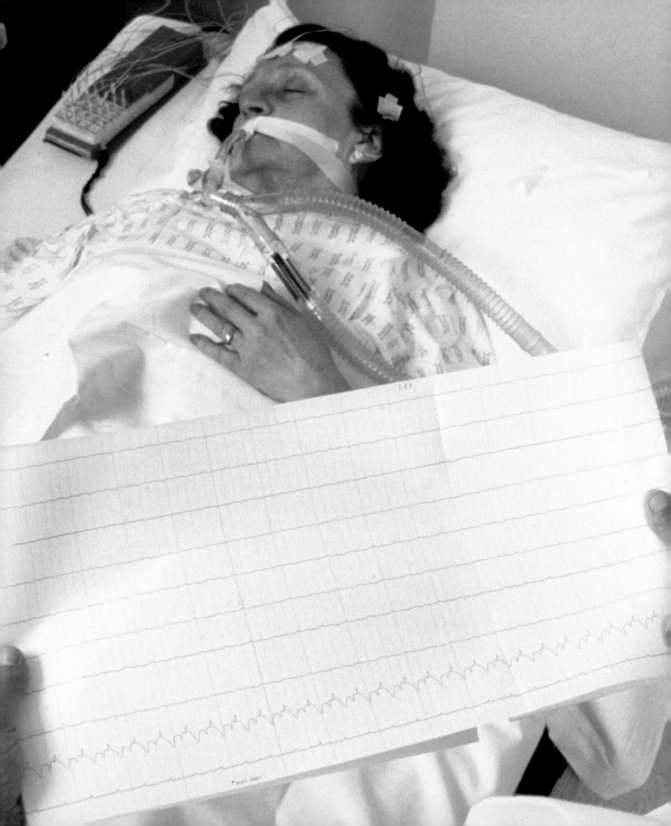

Chapter 4

AT DEATH'S
DOORSTEP

When death is near, the body usually undergoes some standard changes. These changes reflect the internal systems that are breaking down. The national organization known as Hospice is one of several that support those dealing with death. Hospice recognizes two phases in the process of dying. First is the pre-active phase of dying. This continues into the active phase of dying. On average, a patient may spend about two weeks in the pre-active stage of death, followed by approximately three days spent actively dying. These phases, the time they take, and the body changes associated with them are not absolute. The active phase of dying has been known to last as much as two weeks. Diseases affecting one or more of a person's body systems may change the sequence of events in an individual's death.

The Phases of Death

Many of the signals that indicate that a person's body is entering the pre-active phase of dying are related. Overall physical activity and metabolism decrease as the body is shutting down. Because metabolism is slowing, a dying person will typically eat and drink less. They will be sluggish, have general body weakness, and show an increased desire to sleep. Some people recognize their own failing functions and report they feel they are dying.

A nurse checks the decreasing brain activity of a patient in a coma. The failure of one body system can seriously affect other systems, ultimately leading to death.

ASSISTING IN A SMOOTH TRANSITION

Toni Farris, RN, Hospice nurse

While most fields within health care emphasize wellness, I have embraced working with dying people as a privilege. My role is to provide the ultimate environment of comfort and peace for my patients and their families while they go through a very tough phase of living. As a Hospice nurse for eighteen years, one thing I have learned in working with the dying patient is that no two patients leave this world in exactly the same way.

What you see on TV or the movies at the bedside of a dying person does not at all mirror reality. An actor is usually shown to have consciousness right up until the last breath, when profound statements are made to loved ones. In actual deaths, with few exceptions, most people are in a state of unresponsiveness for at least a short period of time before they die, and often for days or more. Through the research of the National Hospice and Palliative Care Organization, nurses and others have forty years of scientific data based on the physiological symptoms of the dying process. These provide us guidelines for helping our patients and their families through a very difficult transition.

The periods of exhaustion may be interrupted by times when the patient becomes agitated. He or she shows signs of body restlessness, mental anxiety, and confusion. The lowered level of nutrients in the body can partly explain these changes in brain activity. The brain needs proper amounts of blood sugar and oxygen to function normally.

The cardiovascular system weakens, in part because the dying patient drinks less liquid. Dehydration sets in. Since blood is mostly water, the result is a lower blood volume. The decrease in blood volume causes lower blood pressure, which slows circulation. Often the heart tries to work harder to move a smaller amount of blood around the body. Blood pressure and blood chemistry grow increasingly abnormal. As a result, the exchange of fluid and nutrients between the blood and other tissues fails to work properly. Accumulating fluids can cause the dying patient's limbs and other parts to swell. The swelling pushes against blood vessel walls and makes it even harder for blood to flow normally.

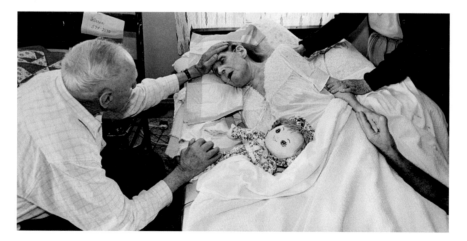

A man comforts his wife during her final hours. Familiar faces, voices, and objects may help ease the fears or confusion of someone who is dying.

Kidney function depends upon adequate blood pressure. As the cardiovascular system weakens and blood pressure drops, kidneys begin to fail. The kidneys clean the blood of some of the wastes from the body's cells. As kidney function slows, toxic wastes build up in the blood. These toxic chemicals poison cells of the nervous system and damage other tissues.

Death is a series of interrelated changes that continue to affect one another. Because body systems are so heavily linked, the failure of one organ or body system puts more stress on others. The body can no longer sustain homeostasis. Massive cell malfunctions occur throughout the body. After a while, a person enters into the active phase of dying.

According to Hospice guidelines, patients who are actively dying may enter a state of coma or semicoma. They seem completely or nearly unresponsive. In addition, the body may become rigid and fixed in one position. At the other extreme, some people who are advancing toward death may experience hallucinations. These may be accompanied by agitation and dramatic changes in personality. In either state of consciousness, breathing and heart activity continue, but obvious changes happen in these functions too.

Breathing becomes increasingly abnormal as the active state of dying progresses. The dying patient usually pauses for an increasing length of time between breaths. This can alternate with cycles of rapid breathing and other irregular patterns of respiration. A normal breathing rate averages about twelve breaths per minute. A dying person's breath rate can range from six (or even less) to fifty breaths a minute. A dying person's mouth may hang open. He or she may cease swallowing and speaking. Breathing sounds and chest movements may become exaggerated. Normal secretions become thickened because of dehydration. The secretions may accumulate because the patient may not be able to swallow or cough. Gurgling sounds often accompany breathing. Periods of ten to thirty seconds or longer can pass without a single breath. Witnesses may believe the patient has died, only to hear the person breathe again after a lengthy pause. The changes taking place during the active phase of dying clearly illustrate that death is a process and only rarely is instantaneous.

During the active stage of death, the cardiovascular system undergoes dramatic and progressive changes. As the dying patient becomes more dehydrated, blood volume continues to decrease, and blood pressure drops. Although the heart tries to move blood through the system, there is simply not enough blood or enough pressure in the blood vessels to function properly.

Normal blood pressure is usually around 120/80 mmHg in a resting adult. (Pressures are measured in mmHg, which stands for "millimeters of mercury." This is based upon the early technology used to measure pressure.) In a blood pressure of 120/80 mmHg, the first number means that when the heart is pumping blood into the cardiovascular system, the force in an artery is 120 mmHg. The second number represents the pressure in an artery between beats of the heart, when the heart is resting.

In an actively dying patient, blood pressure may drop to less than 70/50 mmHg. With such a drop in blood pressure, cells will starve from a lack of nutrients. They will be unable to produce the energy they need and will be poisoned by their own wastes.

Seriously low blood pressure will cause total kidney failure. As dehydration progresses and the kidneys shut down, an actively dying person's urine output will decrease or stop altogether. Toxins may be concentrated in this urine, and it may be red or brown in color.

Survival reflexes send the scarce blood remaining to the most important internal organs. Blood from less active tissues, such as the skin, moves deep into vital organs, such as the heart and lungs. As a result, the limbs of a dying patient can look blotchy, blue, or purple. Because the blood carries much of the body's heat, the dying patient's limbs may feel cold. If the person is still conscious, he or she may experience a loss of feeling in the legs or feet because of the lack of circulating blood in those areas.

The normal heart rate for an average adult is about 72 beats per minute. This can soar to as high as 150 beats per minute in someone who is actively dying. This rate reflects the heart's frantic attempt to move a small amount of blood around the body. The rapid fluttering of the heart is faint, often irregular, and not enough. Aspects of homeostasis are still making vain attempts at correction, but they are completely inadequate.

As voluntary muscles give out, the bowel and bladder may expel their contents. Loss of feces will depend on how long it has been since the person last ate and defecated. If the patient has not eaten for a long time, there will be nothing in the digestive tract to release. When muscle control ceases, the excretion of urine is determined by whether or not enough kidney function remained to produce urine in the bladder. Excretion of wastes is not automatic at death.

In the final stages of the actively dying patient's life, even the vital brain reflexes that control temperature fail. The body feels alternatively cold or feverish. The dying patient's skin may be very dry or slightly moist. Some small metabolic reactions are continuing. However, they are abnormal and not enough to sustain life. The limited metabolic processes use up the small amounts of oxygen and nutrients still in the blood. As circulation fails to deliver life-sustaining blood, the body systems that once worked in harmony finally cease all functions. A life has ended.

Signs That Death Has Occurred

The ways one human recognizes when another has completed the dying process have changed over time. Historical tales and myths tell of people being buried alive when they were actually in a deep coma. Even the tradition in some cultures of laying out the body of the deceased (sometimes called a wake) came about because people needed to be sure that the person was dead. If the seemingly lifeless body was laid out for a period of time and the individual did not "wake," the person was assumed to be dead. Today's heart monitors, brain wave recording devices, and other technological advances can show the inactivity of individual organs as they shut down.

In this 1873 illustration, an Irish family gathers around the coffin of a departed loved one during a wake. In this tradition, friends and family came to the dead person's home to grieve and to share memories of the person's life. If the person did not revive during that time, the funeral proceeded the next day.

Do hair and nails continue to grow after death?

No. Dead cells cannot generate energy, so growth of body tissues is impossible once death has occurred. As soft tissues of the fingers and scalp dry out, they may pull back from fingernail and hair roots. This can expose areas that were covered by skin during life, giving the appearance of new growth.

Have people been buried alive?

Determining death has not always been straightforward, so throughout history people have accidentally been buried alive. Written accounts dating back as far as the sixteenth century, as well as more recent tales from coroner's offices, document these rare incidents. Modern technology, however, allows tests of brain and heart function to confirm that death has occurred.

Do the eyes stay open after death?

Upon death, all muscles of the body relax. This leads to dilated pupils, eyes that remain slightly open, and a slack jaw (because it takes muscle activity to close the eyelids and the mouth). For a funeral, mortuary technicians may place plastic caps beneath the eyelids to help keep them closed and use fasteners that connect the upper and lower jaw to ensure a closed mouth in the deceased.

We have all seen death scenes on television and in movies. These staged versions of the dying process are usually far more dramatic than the actual event. In reality, the signs that death has occurred are simple and predictable. They hold true for sudden deaths as well as those that are expected. They include no breathing, no heartbeat, and the loss of blood pressure and blood movement. As all body muscles relax, the lower jaw typically goes slack and the mouth hangs slightly open. Usually the eyes will be open to some extent, and the eyeballs will be fixed in one spot with dilated (relaxed) pupils.

If the bladder or rectum is full, control over these organs will be lost at death. Because all body muscles relax at death, the deceased person will go limp. Body parts will drop naturally, responding to gravity. Compared to the struggle to get air and the sometimes restless nature of the dying process, the aftereffects of death often look peaceful.

The obvious changes that signal the death of the individual are only part of the story. Those are signs that entire organs, such as the heart, have ceased their functions. The heart failed because a significant number of specific heart cells malfunctioned and died. In turn, the circulatory system failed to deliver oxygen and nutrients to other organs, and they shut down as well. Even when death of the individual seems apparent, some cells in the body are still struggling to maintain function for a very brief period. The body still contains stored nutrients, and some cells even store oxygen, so tissues and cells do not all die at the same moment. (A huge number of cells in and on the body are bacteria that are normally with a person throughout life. These organisms do not die when the body stops functioning.)

Determining when someone is fully and legally dead may be quite difficult, since death is usually a sequence of small events and not instantaneous. Medical technology and artificial feedings can replace failed systems and prolong life beyond its natural limits. All of this contributes to struggles over definitions of what constitutes death. For example, families and medical professionals sometimes find themselves in conflict over patients who are brain dead but whose other vital organs are still functioning. Future technologies may change how we define the death of an individual. Until then, medical and legal debates about quality of life and measurement of death will continue.

Medical issues directly relate to disorder, disease, and ultimately death. But in a society that depends upon laws to maintain order, legal concerns also surround a death. Many people die naturally of disease, suddenly or gradually, whether aware of the disorder or not. On the other hand, death may be caused by something other than a chronic or acute illness. When questions arise about the reason for an individual's death, the legal system steps in to assist medical science.

Some life-and-death issues have been highly publicized and controversial. Terri Schiavo spent fifteen years on artificial life support after a brain injury left her in a persistent vegetative state. Her husband, family, and doctors waged a seven-year legal battle over whether or not life support should continue, since it was clear she would not recover. In 2005 the courts ruled that Terri Schiavo be withdrawn from life support. In this picture, Schiavo's father poses with her portrait.

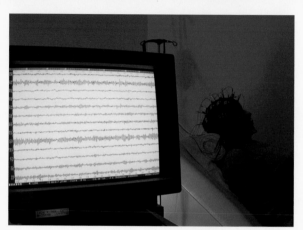

In 1968 a Harvard Medical School committee set forth four criteria for diagnosing when the brain is permanently nonfunctional. To be declared brain dead, a patient must be 1) unreceptive and unresponsive, 2) have no movement and no breathing, 3) exhibit no reflexes, and 4) demonstrate a flat electroencephalogram (EEG). It is recommended that this patient be reexamined twenty-four hours later and show no change.

An electroencephalograph *(above)* records the electrical signals of brain cells. The medical technician places conductors called electrodes on the surface of the patient's scalp. The patient's brain activity produces signals that are recorded as waves, so a flat electroencephalogram signifies an absence of brain function.

A U.S. Presidential Commission studied the medical, legal, and ethical issues surrounding determination of death in 1981. Although this group supported the Harvard criteria, the commission suggested that skilled physicians should be able to use their own judgment and a bedside examination to establish that death has occurred. In some cases, ready access to sophisticated technology, such as an EEG machine, may not be available. A twenty-four-hour waiting period should not be required if death is obvious (particularly if organ donation from the deceased is a possibility). All fifty states have adopted the Uniform Determination of Death Act. It does not specify tests or technology. It simply states that any person who has irreversible loss of circulatory, respiratory, or entire brain functions must be determined to be dead by accepted medical standards.

Chapter 5

MANNER AND CAUSE OF DEATH

Coroners and medical examiners are charged with the legal aspects of deaths that occur in their local area. Because they link medicine and law, these specialists are said to be part of the medicolegal profession. The offices of coroners and medical examiners employ many other specialists. These include pathologists, who study disease; death investigators, who analyze death scenes; and a variety of forensic scientists. The term *forensic* means that something is up for debate or open to legal interpretation. Forensic science involves any chemical, biological, or physical evidence related to criminal acts and crime scenes. Many forensic investigations involve living people who have been victims or have committed crimes. But the primary responsibility of coroners and medical examiners is the investigation of questionable deaths or any loss of life related to illegal actions.

It is the responsibility of the coroner or medical examiner in the jurisdiction (the local area) in which a person dies to assign cause and manner of death. Legally, coroners and medical examiners in the United States have five classifications for what is known as manner of death. These categories are natural deaths, accidental deaths, suicides, homicides, and

A mortuary worker removes a body from cold storage for examination. If investigators suspect that questionable circumstances surround a death, they will move the body to a morgue where the remains can be carefully studied.

Forensic anthropologists examine a skeleton recovered from a crime scene. They will examine the bones to help establish the age, sex, height, and ethnicity of the victim. There may be clues as to how long the person has been dead, as well as evidence of trauma on the bones.

deaths in which the manner can't be determined (unknown). The manner of death relates not to a specific bodily malfunction but more to the circumstances or intentions surrounding a death. From a legal standpoint, all deaths are given both a manner and one or more underlying causes. For example, a death that is ruled natural is one that occurred due to a disorder the person had. The cause of that person's death is the actual disease or problem that ended his or her life. All circumstances surrounding a victim's death may not be fully understood, however, despite the best efforts of the scientists involved. For instance, if a skeleton is found with no apparent signs of foul play, both the manner and cause of death could be recorded as unknown.

A WHO'S WHO OF FORENSIC EXPERTS

There are legal reasons, as well as public health and safety reasons, to analyze how and why people die. In the United States, the systems for investigating deaths vary from state to state, and different titles are used for the professionals involved. For example, a pathologist is a medical doctor who is trained to understand disease and injury. A forensic pathologist performs autopsies at many coroner's and medical examiner's offices. A coroner is usually an elected county official who may or may not be a medical doctor. Coroners in some states may be morticians, emergency medical personnel, dentists, and others who are not physicians. Even in those states that do require coroners to be doctors (Louisiana, North Dakota, Ohio, and Kansas), these physicians do not have to be pathologists. They can be specialists in any field of medicine. In all cases, regardless of a coroner's background, he or she will work closely with a pathologist in analyzing deaths.

The term *medical examiner* has different meanings in different states. Most individuals with that title are physicians appointed by a governmental agency to oversee death investigations. Only some states use this title in their forensic offices.

Death investigators are specific types of forensic crime scene personnel who are trained to assist coroners and medical examiners. They work primarily in heavily populated areas, where many death investigations need to be performed regularly. Some death investigators have credentials in nursing, mortuary science, law enforcement, or emergency medicine. Beyond that they have specialized training that allows them to interpret a death scene and note any important findings that may allow the coroner, medical examiner, or pathologist to better understand the circumstances surrounding a death.

Together, the manner and cause are the coroner's or medical examiner's best evaluation of all the circumstances and body failures involved in a person's death. But as discussed earlier, the body's systems interact and rely upon one another in complex ways. This can make understanding of the cause of death complicated.

Circumstances Surrounding a Death

The manner by which a death occurs is an important legal consideration. A medical professional or death investigator may readily recognize the signs that a death was most likely due to natural causes. And if the death was expected, a coroner will rule the manner of death as "natural" on a death certificate, often without an autopsy, if there were no suspicious circumstances.

An autopsy is a thorough examination of a body after death. It involves opening the body cavities, inspecting and weighing organs, and taking samples of tissues, including blood and other body fluids. A pathologist performs an autopsy. In some places, the coroner or medical examiner may be a pathologist, but not always. (Definitions of who can serve as coroner vary from state to state. A coroner is an elected official, not necessarily a physician.) In cases of unexpected death, a forensic pathologist almost always performs an autopsy, even if there are no signs of foul play. This is done to establish as firmly as possible that the manner of death was natural. The actual cause of death may have been any number of body malfunctions—a sudden heart attack, a stroke from a clogged vessel in the brain, or a blowout in a major artery (an aneurysm)—that can prove fatal.

PRESERVING THE SCENE

Greg Rolfsen and Ed Deters, death investigators

The role of the death investigator is to go to a death scene and serve as eyes and ears for the pathologist. It is our job to bring the surroundings of the body back to the morgue. We collect scientific data that may be helpful in estimating the time of death, such as core liver temperature. Good photography is an invaluable tool that we use to develop the story and help simplify complicated scenes. Plus pictures can be revisited if questions arise after leaving the death scene.

A death investigator must also gather information about the subject's life and circumstances prior to death. We speak with the next of kin and work with the police officers involved. A death investigator asks many questions: Was the victim depressed? When was this person last seen alive? Did the deceased regularly see a doctor and why? What food or drugs may have been consumed before death? Did the victim own a gun?

Death investigation is an interesting and challenging job, in part, because the day-to-day activities are totally unpredictable. However, it can be very difficult to witness the intimate and horrifying extremes of human experience. At many scenes we trespass into the most private parts of people's spaces—their bathrooms, their computers, and frequently their bedrooms. When we leave, it is as if the victim has been violated twice, once by the death and once by the investigation.

ANSWERING QUESTIONS AT THE AUTOPSY TABLE

Lee D. Lehman, PhD, MD, forensic pathologist

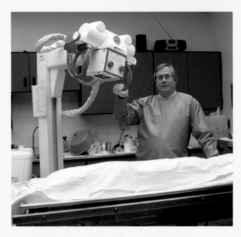

An autopsy changes the body; therefore, before anything else, the pathologist photographs the condition of the body as it came to the morgue. An X-ray machine is used to find foreign bodies, such as bullets or bomb fragments, and to look for broken bones. Trace evidence is collected, for example, foreign hairs or suspected gunshot residue, followed by cleaning of the body.

Once any blood and debris are removed, any injuries on the outside of the body can be seen clearly and photographed. Internal injuries and diseases such as a heart attack, pneumonia, or stroke are found by a procedure similar to exploratory surgery. During the internal examination, injuries to each organ are examined and a small piece (called a biopsy) of each organ is removed and later viewed under a microscope. Blood and tissues are examined by a toxicology laboratory to look for drugs or poisons. To complete the autopsy, a report is made containing all the observations and findings.

Every person and every autopsy is unique. So many different conditions and diseases exist that it is not unusual to find something truly rare during what you think is a routine autopsy. After many years of practice, I still continue to find diseases and injuries I have never encountered before.

Obviously, accidents kill people as well. A coroner or medical examiner will rule the manner of death accidental if there was no intent to cause harm on the part of anyone involved. Of course, risky behavior increases the odds of accidental death. People who drive too fast, drive while intoxicated, take illegal drugs, or engage in other dangerous activities expose themselves to the possibility of accidental death. Clearly, if you never go skydiving from a plane, you can never suffer an accidental death caused by a parachute malfunction. Some accidents are said to be freak accidents, because they are extremely rare and unexpected. They are not the result of risky behaviors or situations. For example, an unknown fault in a common, trusted appliance could cause an accidental electrocution during normal use.

A pathologist performs an autopsy in any case of accidental death. This could be an auto accident or a person found lying in the yard at the base of an upright house ladder. Even in an auto accident in which the driver has clear life-ending injuries, an autopsy may reveal that the person had illegal drugs or alcohol in his or her system. It is also possible that a seizure, a reaction to medication, or a stroke caused the driver to lose control of the vehicle. The victim at the bottom of the ladder may have had a heart attack while climbing up to the roof. The medical examiner must firmly establish what happened in such situations to rule a death as accidental. Combined with a thorough scene investigation, an autopsy can establish that the manner of death was, in fact, accidental.

Some people die because they choose to take their own life. There are many kinds of suicidal deaths. Intentional drug overdoses, gunshots, and sharp wounds are all ways that individuals end their lives. The manner of death is ruled as suicide whenever people willingly inflict harm on themselves with dying as the intended result. In such cases, medicolegal officials will perform an autopsy and undertake a death investigation. Only when all facts—regarding the body, the person's mental state (if known), and the circumstances of the scene—are examined can a coroner or medical examiner rule a death as self-inflicted. It is not unheard of for a murderer to stage a killing to resemble a suicide. So officials must carefully investigate any suspicious death.

Some people who are incurably ill and in great emotional and physical pain may wish to stop their suffering by ending their lives. There has been much social and legal controversy over the practice known as euthanasia (Greek for "good death"). Laws in most of the United States do not allow a medical professional or anyone else to aid another's death in what is known as assisted suicide. Most states hold that no person may end the life of another with intent unless acting in self-defense or in other extreme circumstances. But if a badly injured person is being kept alive solely by medical technology and could not live without such artificial means, the victim's next of kin can legally order medical professionals to turn off life-support machinery. This allows the natural progression of death to take its course. The law does not

This retired doctor does not wish to be kept alive by artificial means. His tattoo informs emergency responders of his intent.

see this as actively taking the person's life. Living individuals can also give these orders ahead of time. They can designate that they do not wish to be revived if their heart or breathing ceases. (This is known as a DNR order, meaning "do not resuscitate.") People can also create living wills, which express their wishes about life-support machinery in the event they become gravely ill.

Homicide is the term used when someone unlawfully kills another person. A coroner or medical examiner declares the manner of death to be homicide if one or more persons deliberately

THE DEATH WITH DIGNITY DEBATE

Euthanasia is the act of assisting a suicide or actively causing the death of a person with a terminal illness. Currently, in the United States, only the states of Oregon (in 1994) and Washington (in 2008) have passed a Death with Dignity Act. The first legal euthanasia occurred in Oregon in 1998, and in the ten years that followed, 341 people used the law to administer their own deaths. The guidelines permit doctors to prescribe a fatal dose of medicine, but only to mentally competent adults with terminal illness and only to residents of the states in which the laws are in place.

These laws are not without social controversy. According to some, they amount to nothing more than state-approved murder in the hands of physicians, whose professional oaths state they should do no harm. Others, however, believe strongly in a person's right to die, and some even think the existing laws allowing euthanasia do not go far enough. Current Death with Dignity guidelines prevent patients suffering with long-term illnesses, such as Alzheimer's and Lou Gehrig's disease, to choose to end their life until they are estimated to be within six months of dying. At that point, they have suffered for years, and few are still able to make their wishes known. No doubt, this legislation in Oregon and Washington will promote ongoing debates in other parts of the country.

ended the life of the deceased and if this killing broke the law. *Murder* and *manslaughter* are legal terms used by the courts to classify homicides. They relate to the type and severity of the criminal act that led to the unlawful death. They are not manners of death.

A homicidal death could be caused by poisoning, suffocation, gunshot trauma, a severe beating, or other injuries. It is the intent that defines a homicide. If a child unknowingly eats a fatal poison or a gun discharges by accident and kills someone, the manner of death is ruled as accidental. In these cases, there was no intent to take a life. The legal system may still become involved. Leaving a toxic substance where a child can easily reach it and carelessly carrying a loaded gun are irresponsible and possibly criminal acts. But those are matters for the courts to decide, not the medical examiner or coroner.

One legal issue concerning homicidal deaths is timing. If one person shoots another and paralyzes him but the victim does not die until years later, the manner of death can still be ruled as a homicide. This is because, even though years may have passed between the gunshot and the death, the intent to kill was present at the time of the shooting. That act finally resulted in the victim's death. An autopsy may be able to clearly link the chain of medical events extending over the years between the criminal act and the death.

Who Is Autopsied, and Who Is Not?

A medicolegal autopsy will be performed in any case of unexpected death. The untimely deaths of apparently young and healthy individuals will always trigger a forensic autopsy to determine the cause. Likewise, if there is any reason to suspect that criminal activity led to a person's death, regardless of age, an autopsy will always be performed as part of the death investigation. Even apparent suicidal deaths will lead to an autopsy to be sure that those who died acted alone to end their lives.

Not everyone who dies at home or in a hospital is autopsied. If the deceased was a patient under a doctor's care, was known to be ill, and was expected to die in the near future from that condition, an autopsy is usually not performed. A forensic autopsy would only be undertaken if something suspicious happened to the patient that could point to the malpractice by medical personnel or indicate abuse or neglect from a caretaker.

In the United States, the decision to perform a forensic autopsy rests with the local coroner or medical examiner. Autopsies may be conducted for other reasons as well. A family member may request an autopsy to confirm a suspected medical condition in a loved one. Some conditions, such as Alzheimer's disease, can be positively diagnosed only through an autopsy of the brain, even though the patient may have suffered the symptoms of the disease for years. These types of medical autopsies are not forensic in nature, so they may be performed at a hospital morgue rather than at a coroner's or medical examiner's facility.

Some families may object to an autopsy for cultural or religious reasons. It may interfere with their beliefs, traditions, or rituals. A coroner or medical examiner can respectfully overrule a family's objection to an autopsy if there is a clear and compelling legal reason to perform it. Different cultures hold varying ideas about what happens to a person after his or her death. Science cannot answer questions about death that relate to the possibility of an afterlife or the presence of a human soul. Such matters are not scientifically testable. Science, however, can explain what happens to the physical body once a person dies.

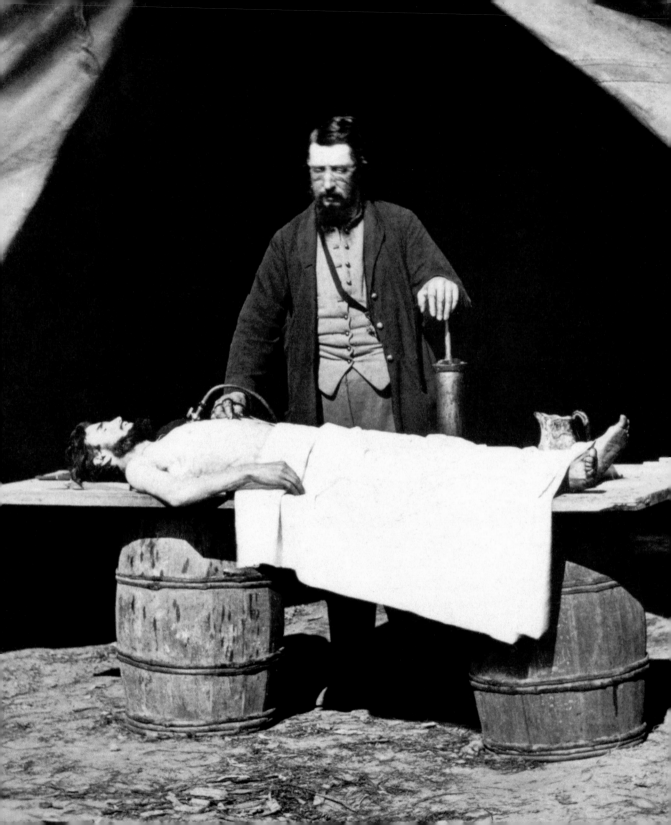

Chapter 6

ALL THAT REMAINS:
POSTMORTEM CHANGES

The process of decomposition is a set of changes that occurs in an organism after its death during a time called the postmortem (after death) period. The branch of science that studies the environmental effects upon an organism once it dies is known as taphonomy. In human bodies, the decomposition process has some common features, but the changes that occur in the minutes and hours after death depend, to some degree, on the cause of death. For instance, an intact body will decompose differently from one destroyed by trauma or fire. A drowning victim's body will be subject to different environments than a body on dry land. The cultural practice of embalming a dead body (as for a funeral) is an attempt to preserve it and prevent decomposition. Thus funeral practices will also greatly determine whether and how decay progresses.

In the broadest sense, there are two overlapping causes for the changes observed in the typical decomposition process. Some decay results because cells and organs are no longer functioning and body tissues are undergoing chemical breakdowns. Other changes during decomposition occur because of the organisms such as bacteria found in and on the living body. These organisms use the energy and nutrients remaining in the dead body.

A doctor embalms the body of a soldier killed in the U.S. Civil War (1861–1865). By treating corpses with chemicals such as arsenic, mercury, turpentine, and alcohol, doctors attempted to slow decomposition so that some war dead could be returned to their families for burial.

MORTUARY SCIENCE AND THE
BUSINESS OF FAMILIES

J. C. Battle III and Lynwood Battle, funeral directors

Embalming is the art and science of temporarily preserving human remains to forestall decomposition and to make them suitable for display at a funeral. The three goals of mortuary science are preservation, sanitization, and restoration of a dead body. Because embalming destroys 98 percent of germs, the process retards decomposition.

The initial steps in the typical embalming include bathing the remains and restoring facial features to a resting appearance. Next blood vessels are opened and a chemical preservative is pushed through the cardiovascular system. Hollow organs are emptied and chemically treated, and the operation sites in the body are sewn closed. Hair is shampooed, skin moisturizers are applied, and the remains are posed in a funeral posture.

Our grandparents started J. C. Battle & Sons Funeral Home in 1933, at the height of the Great Depression. They wanted to be in business for themselves and saw mortuary science as a good way to serve the community. We are now in our seventy-fifth year, and the third generation of morticians is operating the firm. We not only take care of the body after death, but we also serve the living. This begins with the first call from the family and continues through the funeral service and final disposition of the remains. We still consider service to families as a high calling.

Whether and how decomposition occurs is largely determined by the temperature of the surroundings and the activity of organisms such as bacteria and insects that feed off the corpse. These two agents of decay are interrelated. A frozen body will not decompose because insects and most bacteria cannot reproduce nor thrive in freezing temperatures. If a dead body is outdoors in an environment that is at or below freezing, larger organisms, such as carnivorous animals, may try to feed off a corpse. But these animals are scavenging the nutrients of the body rather than acting as agents of decomposition.

Livor, Algor, Odor, and Rigor

At death the heart no longer pushes blood onward, so the blood stops circulating. Like any liquid, blood will respond to the pull of gravity. Blood will begin to settle in the lowest body regions. If the deceased is lying on his or her back, blood will move toward the vessels of the back. If the body is face down, blood will collect in the tissues on the front of the body.

Often blood will not gather in an area of skin where something is pressing on a body part. For example, the skin may not fill with blood beneath a tight waistband. A pale impression may be left on the skin if some object, such as a gun or a book, was lodged between the victim and the floor. This pooling of blood and the patterns it produces may provide important clues in a forensic investigation. It can reveal information about the body's position at the time of death or whether the body was moved after death.

Scientists refer to this stage of blood pooling as livor mortis. The settling of blood is typically visible on the skin's surface about one hour after death. The patterns on the skin that result

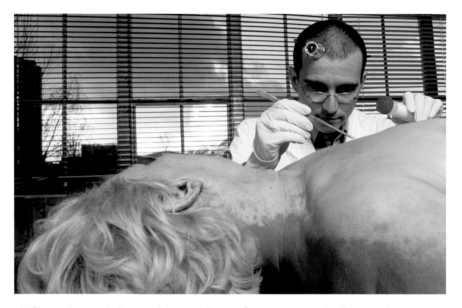

A forensic specialist gathers evidence from a recently deceased person. The corpse's skin shows the discoloration of blood pooling, called livor mortis, on the neck and shoulders.

from livor mortis are firmly established within about eight hours after death. After that, they will not change even if the body is moved. Coloring from livor mortis usually remains until more advanced decomposition completely discolors the body.

At the same time that blood stops moving, a cooling stage of decomposition begins. In the human body (and that of other warm-blooded animals), metabolic processes and muscle action generate body heat. Because these activities stop at death, the body begins to cool. This cooling stage is known scientifically as algor mortis. Cooling will depend on the air temperature around the body, whether the deceased is indoors or out, and how the body is covered. The loss of body heat will take place faster if the surrounding air is cold. Heat loss is slower in a hot environment. By comparing the body temperature to the air temperature at a death scene, forensic investigators can estimate how long a person has been dead. That is true at least until the body temperature finally equals that of its surroundings.

Livor mortis and algor mortis are two of the early processes in the typical sequence of decay. Breakdown occurs on the cellular level too. From a cellular standpoint, death occurred because cells lacked the energy necessary to maintain homeostasis. Without these balancing acts, there is a total collapse of normal function. For instance, the membranes of dead cells no longer keep the proper balance of chemicals outside and inside the cell. Cells may rupture and spill out their contents. Cell organelles that once held enzymes will break open. The enzymes will digest the very cells that used to contain them. This process is known as autolysis. Clearly, death doesn't mean that all chemical reactions have ceased. Instead, new combinations of chemicals interact as organelles, cells, tissues, and organs break down. This is no longer the chemistry of a living body. It is the chemistry of decomposition.

Unless something interrupts this progression of decay, such as embalming, cremation, or refrigeration at the morgue, internal chemical changes will continue. These include spontaneous biochemical reactions. Existing chemical bonds break and new bonds form within decaying tissue. Two particularly interesting molecules result from the decomposition of human tissues (and those of other mammals). These molecules have been named cadaverine and putrescine because of their association with dead bodies in a putrefied (decomposed) state. Scientists have discovered that these two chemicals cause much of the smell associated with decaying animals. Perhaps you have walked or driven past a decomposing mammal by the roadside and noticed this pungent odor of death.

Another change that occurs following livor mortis and algor mortis is stiffening of the muscle tissue in a human or animal corpse. Muscle activity is a living body function that obviously requires energy. During normal muscle action, a series of carefully controlled chemical bonds occurs inside muscle cells to cause the muscles to contract. When muscle cells no longer have an energy source, they lose control over their internal chemistry. This leads to the chemical bonds of contraction forming spontaneously among the proteins inside muscle cells. The result is a state of muscle rigidity known as rigor mortis.

How quickly rigor mortis happens depends on the amount of available energy in the body's muscle cells at the time of death. If a person ran a marathon and then died from a heart attack, rigor mortis would set in rapidly. This is because that person had used up most of his or her available energy while running. Rigor mortis would set in more slowly if a person had been sleeping and had a fatal heart attack.

Under typical conditions, rigor mortis sets in within a few hours, but it does not last indefinitely. Usually on the second day after death—or as late as the third—rigor mortis ends and the muscles resume a lax state. Decomposition will continue unless the body is embalmed or kept cold. If the body is not preserved in some way and decay proceeds, the soft tissues of the corpse continue to break down. As they do, organs and muscle become softer. They give off more odor as biochemical changes continue. As the underlying layers of tissue become slippery and gooey, the discolored outer layer of the skin may begin to slip off in pieces. The hair may come off the scalp. In some cases, extremities and edges of body parts—lips, ears, fingers, and toes—may dry out. Outward features become distorted. A person's features may become difficult to identify.

During the first few days after a person's death, many of the signs of decomposition are due to chemical reactions occurring within the body's tissues. A lack of usable energy and the failure of normal processes will drastically alter the biochemistry of the body. Old molecules break down, and new ones form. Although dead cells are unable to use energy, body tissues are still warehouses of nutrients that can be used by other life-forms. Some decomposition processes are the result of the millions of bacterial cells that live in and on the human body.

Living on the Dead

A great amount of potential energy remains in the tissues of the deceased. This is because some body processes take in and store nutrients during life. In addition, all chemical bonds, including those that make up body structures, are a source of energy.

Living cells use a variety of molecules to produce the energy needed for body functions. During life, an organism's diet provides compounds such as carbohydrates, fats, and proteins. The body uses some of the chemicals in food to make cells and tissues. So some of what is eaten becomes part of the body's structures. Because humans and other animals eat only from time to time (as in several meals a day), excess nutrients are often stored in the tissues. Between meals the chemicals necessary for life processes may be borrowed from the stored nutrients.

Many tissues are rich reserves of energy, such as the fat stores beneath our skin. Even muscle tissue is a potential source of energy, because it is made of a variety of proteins. But even though a cell may contain or be surrounded by fat or protein, body cells must also have oxygen to make energy. After death the respiratory system no longer brings in oxygen. So even though the tissues of a dead body are a source of stored energy, the body's cells can no longer use it.

A human body carries more bacterial cells living on it and in it than the total number of cells belonging to its own tissues and organs. Bacterial cells are much smaller than the cells of animal tissue. Any body surface that is exposed to the outside environment—the outside of the skin or an internal surface such as the mouth—has bacteria living on it. Most of these bacteria are part of a person's normal interaction with the world. They are usually not harmful. Some are actually beneficial. Of course, disease-causing microorganisms can also be found on body surfaces.

The human digestive tract contains a tremendous number of bacteria. From the mouth to the stomach, within the intestines, and especially in the colon and rectum, certain types of bacteria live in harmony with the human host. The bacteria living in the large intestine aid digestion. They break down the fibers found in plants that humans cannot digest on their own. These bacteria produce gases as a by-product of their breakdown of these fibers. The gas that may be associated with eating beans, broccoli, cabbage, and other high-fiber foods does not actually come from these foods. It comes from the bacteria that feed off them in the large intestine.

The life cycles of these bacteria do not end when a person dies. During life, body defense mechanisms and good personal hygiene usually hold bacterial numbers in check. They keep bacteria living only on body surfaces to which they are adapted. Intact skin and the mucous membranes that line the body tracts prevent bacteria from reaching the bloodstream or deeper tissues. White blood cells destroy invaders before their numbers get too large, defending people from bacteria that make it past the protective barriers. Like all other body processes, however, these defenses are functions of living tissues.

After death, defense mechanisms break down, allowing bacterial cells to multiply and take over. Bacteria reproduce quickly, some creating several generations within a single hour. So their populations increase dramatically.

In a dead body, long before the intact skin decays to let in surface bacteria, the vast population of bacteria normally living

THE MICROORGANISMS THAT LIVE WITH US

An enormous number of microscopic organisms, such as bacteria and fungi, live in harmony on the various surfaces of the human body. Our normal body defenses and hygiene, as well as competition among these life-forms, keep these populations under control. Some of these species benefit us, but others can cause disease if their numbers increase or if they colonize body surfaces where they are not normally present. Some also contribute to the decomposition process after body defenses cease to function.

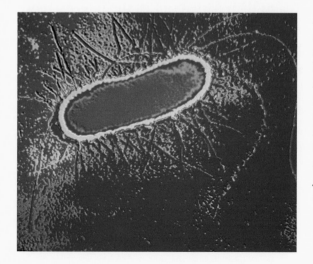

Many kinds of bacteria are normally present in the human body. E. coli (left) live in the lower gastrointestinal tract where they aid our digestion. However, E. coli can cause serious infections and even death if they grow elsewhere in the body.

in the intestines grows to extraordinary numbers. Gut bacteria are anaerobic. That means they do not require oxygen. They can continue to use the body's nutrients, even though respiration has ended and no oxygen is available. As they feed, they continue to create gases, primarily a gas called methane. The anaerobic bacteria keep reproducing, metabolizing, and producing gas in the intestines. Over time, the bacterial gases in a decomposing body cause the intestines to swell. This gas is the reason that dead animals, including humans, tend to bloat in their abdomen in the days after death. This is also why a person who drowns might sink at first but rise to the water's surface days later as the gas inside the body increases.

Distinct environmental conditions favor different types of bacteria. For example, some anaerobic bacteria thrive underwater. Therefore, a body will decompose differently on land than it will in the water. A change in the conditions around a body or in the body itself will change the kinds of bacteria on and in it. Gut bacteria need the right conditions for their growth, including a moist environment lacking in oxygen. A bloated animal carcass may actually burst or tear open and then flatten out as the internal gases are released. Some varieties of gut bacteria will begin to die off as they are exposed to air. They will be replaced by other bacteria, in and on the body and in the environment, which thrive in the presence of oxygen. They are known as aerobic bacteria.

The organisms involved in decomposition also include some one-celled creatures known as protists. Like bacteria, these are a diverse group of microscopic organisms. Some protists feed on bacteria and play important roles in breaking down dead tissues, particularly in damp or underwater environments. Together, many types of bacteria and protists provide the base of the food chain for other living organisms.

One entire kingdom of organisms is made up of decomposers. These are the fungi, which range from microscopic varieties to large mushrooms. This group includes a great diversity of molds, mildews, yeasts, and more. Only some fungi feed off the bodies of dead animals. (Many break down decaying plant matter and return nutrients to the soil.) But fungi are some of nature's best recyclers. Some types of molds can live inside a casket and can even form on embalmed human tissue.

Insects and Other Animal Scavengers

Countless numbers of living organisms—large and small—have existed throughout our planet's history. Earth would be covered with dead and decaying tissues from once-living things if not for the presence of decomposers. Essentially, these creatures take from the dead to feed the living. Except for plants and other organisms (like some bacteria) that can capture energy directly from the sun, all living things must feed off others to sustain life. Those bacteria, protists, and fungi that feed off dead and decaying matter are specialized to recycle the leftovers of a body that is no longer functional. Some animals, especially certain varieties of insects, also live off the remains of dead organisms and have a role in decomposition.

Scientists call insects that feed off decaying flesh necrophagous (*necro* means "dead," and *phagous* means "to eat"). These corpse-eating species will rapidly break down soft tissues. Necrophagous insects are dependent upon finding and inhabiting animal remains for some part of their life cycle.

Flies that feed off decaying flesh are usually the first insects to arrive at a dead body. But when adult flies circle around and land on a body, they are not feeding. These are females looking for a place to deposit their eggs. In the early part of a fly's life cycle, an egg hatches into a legless larval form known as a maggot. The larvae must develop in a moist location. Females often choose body openings, or orifices, in which they lay their eggs. These include natural openings, such as the mouth, nose, eyes, anus, and female reproductive tract. Flies may also deposit their eggs in wounds. In the early stages of decomposition, the presence of fly larvae in a place other than a natural body opening often means that the body was damaged in some way at that spot.

Fly eggs appear as small clusters of white crust or dust. The eggs hatch relatively quickly, usually in about a day, and tiny larvae emerge and begin to feed. Maggots have mouthparts that allow them to pierce the body and extract liquids and nutrients from the corpse. They feed and grow within the dark, wet confines of the decaying body. When they reach a certain size, the maggots will usually migrate from the corpse to a dark but drier spot. If the body is outdoors, the larvae will wriggle away and burrow into the soil. Indoors, however, the maggots may have only clothing, carpeting, or other furnishings in which to hide.

Once they migrate from the body, the larvae become still. Their outer body covering hardens into a shell-like case called a pupa. Inside the firm protection of the pupa, the larval body transforms into an adult fly. This transformation is called metamorphosis. The adult fly emerges from its pupa and begins the reproductive phase of its life. The total span of time from egg to adult fly is normally a few weeks.

Scientists called entomologists study insects. They have learned that necrophagous flies have extraordinary abilities

A blowfly lays eggs on animal tissue (above). A larva (inset) hatches from a fly egg to feed on the dead tissue. Depending on the temperature, the larva will usually grow and reach adulthood within weeks. Scientists can study the insects on a body and estimate how much time has passed since death. Larvae might also carry traces of drugs or poisons that were present in the body at death.

to detect the chemicals given off in the very early stages of animal decomposition. They can easily find bodies out in the open when they sense death. They also can fly great distances and squeeze into very small openings in buildings and vehicles or down into soil. Forensic entomologists have learned to match the life cycle of flies with the air temperature to estimate how long a person has been dead. The scientists must have samples of the insects from a corpse, the precise time and place those insects were collected, and the climate data from that area for the period just before the insects were collected. Maggots from a body can even be mashed and chemically tested to see if drugs or other toxins were present in a body during decomposition.

Flies are only the first part of the insect story in decomposition. As the soft tissues of the body begin to dry out, flesh-eating beetles often move in to inhabit and feed off a corpse. Some beetles are very specific body feeders. For example, some prefer only skin. And while flies and beetles inhabit a dead body, other creatures often prey on these insects. Ants may steal fly eggs, spiders may set up webs to ensnare flies, and birds and raccoons may pick maggots off a corpse.

Many types of scavengers will visit a corpse, and their variety will depend upon the environment and possibly the time of year. If a dead body is in water, fish, crabs, and turtles may pull flesh off the remains. When a body is on land, many types of scavenging mammals, including bears, coyotes, raccoons, opossums, rats, and even dogs and cats may feed off it. Birds such as buzzards and vultures also feed off animal carcasses. Scavengers and large carnivores can do serious damage to remains—scattering body parts, eating parts of the corpse, or chewing on bones. This can greatly complicate the forensic analysis of a body and a crime scene.

Temperature and Decay

Temperature can greatly affect how—and even whether—decay occurs. If the body is in a frigid environment, especially below freezing, decomposition will slow or even stop altogether. A frozen body will remain largely in the same state and position it was in when freezing occurred.

STUDYING DECOMPOSITION—
THE BODY FARM

In late 1980, on an acre (0.4 hectares) of land behind the University of Tennessee's Medical Center in Knoxville, a 16-square-foot (1.5 square-meter) area was paved and enclosed by a fence. This was the humble beginning of the most famous decomposition facility in the world. It is commonly known as the Body Farm *(above)*. Dr. Bill Bass, a professor at the university and the forensic anthropologist for the Tennessee Bureau of Investigation, recognized the need to study decomposition in a scientific way. He created the Body Farm as a means to do so.

In spring of 1981, the first donor body arrived at the site. It was intensively observed by Dr. Bass and his doctoral student, Bill Rodriguez. At times Rodriguez sat in a folding chair, taking notes and photos, with netting around his head to keep the flies out of his own mouth, nose, eyes, and ears. This initial research led to scientifically classifying the stages of decomposition and documenting the insects involved.

Since that time, remains have been buried, submerged in water, wrapped in plastic, closed in a car's trunk, and placed in many other realistic forensic settings by scientists. Observing decomposition at the site has generated methods to assess the age, sex, ethnicity, and stature of unknown individuals. Although considered controversial by some, the Body Farm has continued to expand and contribute to a clearer understanding of postmortem changes. The facility has grown to cover about 2.5 acres (1 hectare) and receives about 120 bodies annually.

Some organisms can resume life after an extended period of freezing if they are frozen intentionally and under very controlled conditions. Frozen human embryos can be held in storage for future implantation. Cryogenics is the science of freezing materials, including living tissues, at extremely low temperatures and studying the effects on them. Some scientists have investigated cryopreservation as a means of holding tissues, organs, and even whole bodies in a frozen state from which they might be brought back to life at a later time. This is an attempt to avoid all the processes of decomposition.

The speed and progress of decay is very different when a body decomposes in extremely hot conditions. High temperatures can be accompanied by lots of moisture, as in a rain forest, or by

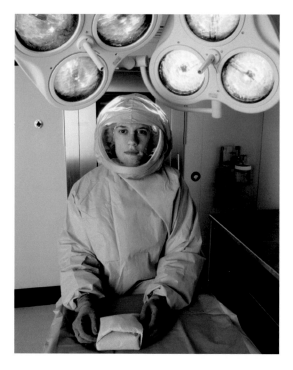

A researcher holds a package of cryogenically preserved human tissue. Scientists must use strict sterile techniques while processing and handling body tissues that have been preserved for future use by freezing.

THAWING AND RAISING THE DEAD

Throughout history, people have wondered if humans can be frozen and brought back to life—perhaps at a time when the illness that caused their death could be cured. Even Benjamin Franklin wrote about this tempting fantasy. Placing a dead human in a state of cryonic suspension was first attempted in California in 1967, but no one has ever been successfully revived from a frozen state. Without the proper chemical protection, freezing damages cell structure and function. Persons are required to be legally dead before being frozen, so the problems that led to their death further decrease the chances that they could be revived successfully.

In extremely cold natural environments, living organisms—such as some insects, fish, amphibians, and reptiles—create chemicals that protect their tissues from freezing. Whether in the laboratory or in nature, however, successful cryopreservation requires specific and controlled processes to take place in healthy tissues. These are ways to protect life, not a means of cheating death.

very low humidity, as in a desert. The temperature and amount of humidity determine the types of organisms that live in an environment. These include the varieties of insects, scavengers, and other decomposers. In an environment of low humidity and near constant temperature, a body may actually dry out and become mummified rather than decompose. Natural mummification is often seen in desert environments. It can also occur in caves, where conditions are relatively constant year-round. Such natural mummies will have dried-out skin, stiff muscles, and dehydrated soft tissues still adhering to the skeleton. Many organisms that aid in decomposition have a hard time feeding off dried tissues. A body that becomes mummified may last a very long time.

This mummy comes from a remote desert in western China. Extremely dry conditions preserved her hair, skin, and clothes for thousands of years.

Death to Dust?

When all the soft tissues—skin, muscle, and internal organs—have fully decomposed, all that remains is a skeleton. Bones and teeth are the most durable parts of the body and can last for a very long time. (If bones and teeth become fossilized by minerals in the environment, they can last indefinitely.) Even the skeleton, however, can break down over time. Soils containing high acid levels can dissolve the minerals in bones, and the bones will crumble. Long before that happens, carnivores might chew on the bones to obtain the minerals and energy-rich bone marrow they contain. Even rodents gnaw on bones to sharpen their teeth.

The thought of animals feeding off a decomposing body, especially a human body, will seem unpleasant to many people. But these organisms are performing a very important role in nature by cleaning up the debris of death. It makes no difference to bacteria, flies, turtles, rats, hyenas, or vultures whether a body belonged to a human or some other creature. The existence of these feeders—like that of all living creatures—is dependent on finding nutrition. Most of the nutrients in our bodies come from the foods we eat, and in death, our bodies may become food for others. As nutrients and energy cycle through the environment, one creature's misfortune may be another organism's survival.

Although not all life-forms feed directly off dead and decaying flesh, all do rely—at least indirectly—on the decomposition that happens in the environment. Organisms that are decomposers reintroduce the chemicals in dead organisms into the living world. Without decomposers there would be no nutrient-rich soil in which plants grow. Plant life, in turn, directly feeds plant-eating herbivores. Plants indirectly feed carnivores when these meat-eating animals eat the herbivores. Food webs in nature involve recycling energy and nutrients from one organism to another. Even in a human, all molecules not present in the original sperm and egg cells that formed a living creature were borrowed from the environment through breathing and eating. It is completely natural and necessary for organisms to feed off one another. And in this way, there is truly life after death.

Chapter 7

DEATH BENEFITS:
LIFE AFTER DEATH

Beliefs and traditions regarding life after death have always varied among spiritual, religious, and cultural groups. Stories about ghosts are found in the mythology and folklore of societies around the world. Halloween and Día de los Muertos (Day of the Dead) are only two of the many traditional customs that celebrate death, mortality, and the spirits of the departed. An extraordinary variety of funeral rituals around the world exist to honor the passing of the dead and, in some cases, to preserve their bodies.

Philosophers, writers, and other curious individuals have explored the mysteries of death and the possibility of an afterlife. They have attended séances and other attempts to contact spirits. Individuals who have been revived after a temporary state of death report seeing powerful images during their near-death experiences. In the end, science cannot evaluate ideas that are not testable, including whether some form of spiritual existence continues after life ends. Nevertheless, in scientific terms, there is definitely life after death. It is seen in the bacteria, insects, and scavengers that inhabit and recycle the bodies of the dead.

Typical funeral practices, such as embalming and cremation, do not return nutrients to the soil. Cremation incinerates a

A man wearing a skull mask visits a statue of Mary, the mother of Jesus, during a Día de los Muertos celebration in Los Angeles, California. Many customs around the world exist to honor the dead and often include supernatural or religious traditions.

body, leaving only bone ash as residue. Embalming prevents bacterial decomposition and renders tissues unsuitable to most organisms. Placing human remains in a modern casket for burial in a concrete vault makes them unreachable by most life-forms that would promote decay. Attempts to preserve the dead extend as far back as ancient Egyptian mummification. Preservation of the body has been considered one way to allow the human body to endure into the future. The reasons behind such cultural practices have varied through history. In modern times, most people decide during their life how they wish their body to be treated after death. Some people view donating their bodies to science as a way to live on into the future.

Where the Dead Teach the Living

Death can contribute to life when scientists study the bodies of those who have died. Examinations of the cells, tissues, and organs of the dead help scientists better understand a variety of diseases. Medical autopsies, combined with the medical histories of patients, allow health-care specialists to advance the care and treatment of a broad range of human disorders. In this way, the dead help the living and promote the progress of medicine.

Most medical students, physical therapy students, and many other health-care professionals learn about human anatomy by studying a cadaver. Generally, a cadaver is a dead body that is intended for dissection and scientific study. Reputable body donation programs have sprung up during the past century to provide cadavers for a variety of scientific and educational needs. Through these programs, individuals sign over their physical remains so that after they die, medical professionals can receive hands-on training in human anatomy.

A BODY OF KNOWLEDGE

D.J. Lowrie Jr., PhD; Efrain Miranda, PhD; Wan Lim, PhD; and Bruce Giffin, PhD, anatomy professors

Although all human bodies are similar, each is also unique in many ways. It is impossible to truly appreciate the wonder and complexity of the human form without studying an actual body. We are eternally grateful to those who donate their bodies for this cause.

A cadaver serves as a first patient to health-care professionals who are in training. As students discuss their findings and consider pathologies, they begin to learn the science of diagnosis. Discoveries of cancers, medical devices, and surgical scars help show the students the medical path ahead of them. They realize how remarkable and resilient the human body is when they see how some people lived with so much disease.

Initially, it takes a while for students to adjust to the dissection, especially when working on areas such as the face and hands. Eventually, the students come to realize that the individual they are learning from is a human being with a family and a personal history. In other words, that this dead body once had a full life. Studying a cadaver is an intimate act that illustrates the humanity in death. Death is seen as an end, but for the cadavers it is the beginning of their roles as teachers.

SUPERVISING CADAVERS AND ASSISTING THEIR FAMILIES

Gina M. Burg, body donation program manager

In the average year, our body donation program receives 360 to 370 bodies. That's just about one per day. These are generally older people, usually with ages in the 80s and 90s. Donations are higher among females, and more Caucasians bequeath their bodies to our program than individuals from other ethnic groups. We are a nonprofit organization, and donors receive no compensation. Most of the bodies received are used to teach medical and physical therapy students.

Once the death of a registered donor occurs, the family arranges transportation through a funeral home or ambulance service. The body is taken to a mortuary college for embalming and then transferred to our facility within a few days. We will use the body for teaching or other research anywhere from about six months to several years after it is received. How and when the body is used depends on the condition of the body and what courses have need for cadavers.

After study, each donor is individually cremated, and the ashes are either returned to the family or buried in our gravesite at a local cemetery. Throughout this process, I provide compassion and support to the families of the deceased. Each year I help plan and host our annual memorial service at which about five hundred people come to celebrate the lives of our generous donors. That is the most gratifying part of my job!

When someone makes the choice to donate his or her body, this person enters into a contract that allows the body to be taken for scientific purposes upon their death. This agreement is kept by the donor's next of kin, his or her doctor, and the body donation facility. The agreement usually doesn't specify the exact purpose of such after-death studies. Sometimes, though, a donation may be for a particular type of research, as when a donor suffers from a rare condition. Occasionally, the body of the deceased is not embalmed before being used in research. This might occur when a new surgical device or artificial joint needs to be tested on a fresh cadaver. More often, however, the donated corpse is transported to an embalming facility for preservation. Sometimes the body goes to a school of mortuary science where future funeral directors learn embalming techniques. Then it may be stored until it is needed for dissection in the gross anatomy laboratory.

In studies of anatomy, the term *gross* means "large," not disgusting. It refers to structures that can be seen without the aid of a microscope. Students studying anatomy usually do a full dissection of the human body, region by region. For instance, when students examine the chest in the gross anatomy laboratory, they study the skin, muscles, bones, nerves, and organs in the chest region. They use scalpels to open skin flaps. They view chest muscles and then cut them away to look at the rib cage. Using an electric saw to open the chest cavity, they study the heart, lungs, and major vessels and nerves of the area. The students can remove specific organs and dissect them to see their internal structure in more detail.

During cadaver dissection, students will also see any obvious diseases present when the person died. Gross anatomy students

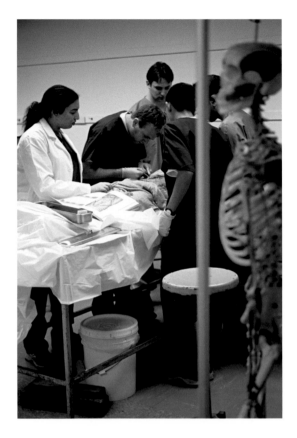

Medical students study a cadaver during an anatomy class.

may find arteries of the heart that are hardened and narrowed by fatty deposits in a cadaver, even though the person was not known to have had heart disease. In that sense, cadaver dissection is much like an autopsy.

Sometimes a person who has elected to donate his or her body dies suddenly in a way that was not foreseen by his or her doctor (such as in an auto accident). Then the body of that individual would not be used for cadaver dissection. In those cases, the medicolegal system would take over that death, and a forensic autopsy would be performed instead.

MESSAGE FROM A
FUTURE CADAVER

Rosemarie Murray,
body donor

I have decided to donate my body to medical science because I think it is the last worthwhile thing on earth I can do. Students can learn much from reading, but there is nothing like hands-on experience. I wonder what my body will tell others about my life.

My family health history is mixed. My dad died of a blocked artery in his heart when he was only fifty-six. Dad knew he was sickly and told Mom he'd never live to see my younger brother and me grow up, and he was right. On the other hand, my mom was healthy, never took much medicine, and lived to be ninety-nine years old.

As for me, I have high blood pressure and high cholesterol, but that is under control with medication. My life included having six children and a husband who was handicapped with severe arthritis. I guess because I worked so hard, I ended up having both knees and hips replaced. Other than that, I feel mighty blessed. I watch my diet and go to a warm water exercise class a couple times a week. If I could talk to the medical students or scientists who will someday study my body I would tell them, "You just have one body, take good care of it."

Throughout history a variety of cultures (including some countries in the modern world) considered it illegal to dissect human beings to gain anatomical knowledge. Ancient Egyptian medical practitioners were permitted to examine cadavers. But by classical Greek and Roman times, or around twenty-five hundred years ago, cutting apart a human body was illegal. In Rome in the second century A.D., the physician Galen attempted to document human anatomy by dissecting apes and pigs. In the sixteenth century, the famous Flemish anatomist Vesalius dissected human remains. He created an accurate atlas of human anatomy that contradicted many of Galen's long-held misconceptions.

By the eighteenth century, many schools of medicine, such as those in the United States and Great Britain, recognized the need to see the internal structure of the body to better understand its workings. Many of the schools employed grave robbers, known as resurrection men, to visit cemeteries by night and dig up recent burials. Undertakers and church officials were sometimes bribed to remove bodies from their caskets and substitute sand before burial. Executed criminals and unclaimed corpses from morgues and hospitals were often used for anatomy studies too. Dissections took place in an auditorium full of people (sometimes including the general public), who observed the process. Before embalming was common, dissections were conducted only in the colder months to slow decomposition. Eventually, cadavers were heavily embalmed, using chemicals such as tar, beeswax, salt, turpentine, arsenic, mercury, rum, and more recently formaldehyde. By preserving them, scholars were able to use the cadavers for longer periods, so they needed fewer of them. As recently as 1912, twelve states in the United States had no legal means to obtain bodies for dissection.

Autopsies performed for legal reasons at a medical examiner's or coroner's office can also benefit science as well as society. Forensic pathologists, chemical analysts known as toxicologists, crime scene investigators, and other forensic laboratory scientists work together to establish the cause and manner of a person's death. When they identify how someone died, justice can be served or suspicions can be laid to rest. Their thorough analyses of unexpected or accidental deaths might also identify toxins in the environment or faulty products that need to be taken off the market. Studying the victims of crimes, accidents, suicides, and mass disasters can advance law enforcement and help protect society.

When Death Gives Life

Through their role in educating future health-care professionals, cadavers may indirectly serve living patients. But there are other, far more immediate ways in which the dead help the living. These include tissue donation and organ donation.

Tissue donation involves removing body tissues for transfer to another person. Not all tissues donated come from the dead. Many types of tissues and even some organs can be transplanted from one living person to another. Blood donation and bone marrow transplants are relatively common. Sometimes people even donate tissue back to themselves, such as when they bank some of their own blood before a planned surgery. A body will reject foreign tissue that does not have similar cell membrane proteins. Receiving one's own tissues greatly lessens the chance for rejection of the transplanted tissue or organ. When donation to self is not possible, some of the best tissue and organ matches come from a close relative. A sibling may choose to donate a kidney or even part of a lung to a brother or sister

ORGAN DONATION IN THE UNITED STATES

The first kidney transplant occurred between a living donor and a recipient in 1954. It was not until 1966 that a kidney was removed from a deceased donor and transplanted into a living recipient. In 2008 in the United States, 7,985 deceased donors and 6,213 living ones resulted in 27,958 organ transplant surgeries. The deaths of these 7,985 donors allowed the transplantation of 21,745 organs. Despite this generosity, 6,229 patients died awaiting a suitable organ donation and transplant surgery. In 2009 more than 102,000 people were on waiting lists for a variety of organs.

Organ(s) Transplanted	Number
Kidney	16,514 (5,963 from living donors)
Liver	6,318 (249 from living donors)
Heart	2,163
Lung	1,478
Kidney and pancreas	836
Pancreas	437 (one from a living donor)
Intestine	185
Heart and lung	27

Based on data from 2008 from the U.S. Department of Health and Human Services, Health Resources and Services Administration and the Organ Procurement and Transplantation Network

who needs it. Because humans have two kidneys and lungs, both the donor and the recipient can hope to have a normal life with one kidney or a partial lung.

Tissue and organ donations from a deceased person, however, usually go to a complete stranger. People can designate themselves as organ donors. Should they die, especially unexpectedly, these people have agreed in advance that some or all of their usable tissues and organs may be donated to needy recipients. Although procedures vary from state to state, many states keep donor registries on file. They might also make a place on driver's licenses for potential donors to make note of their wishes.

Time is an important consideration in organ donation, since once death has occurred, many vital organs, such as the heart and lungs, rapidly become unsuitable for donation because of the changes during body decomposition. Corneas (part of the surface of the eyes), bone tissue, and skin grafts can be transplanted from the deceased to the living up to about twenty-four hours after death.

Other types of organ donations usually come from individuals who have suffered an accident that caused them to be brain dead. The heart and respiratory functions of these individuals are artificially prolonged by machines and medications. This is different from being in a coma or otherwise unresponsive, as in a vegetative state. Brain death means that all vital reflexes have ceased and the brain lacks all activity. Such a person cannot be revived by any means. An absolute lack of brain function is indicated by pupils of the eyes that do not respond to light, an absence of blinking even when the surface of the eye is stroked, no response to pain, and no electrical signals coming from the brain. Declaring a person to be brain dead often requires independent evaluations from two medical doctors, perhaps hours apart.

Obviously, any organs that are badly damaged in a serious accident are unusable. However, even older people or those with a chronic disease may be able to donate one or more organs. Transplantation specialists analyze the genetic profile of a potential donor and the condition of his or her body to determine when a match is suitable. Tissues and organs harvested from

A surgeon prepares a donor heart for transplantation.

brain-dead individuals are kept in controlled temperature and chemical conditions. Vital organs must be transplanted within hours after removal. Despite this critical time element, organs are sometimes flown across the country for lifesaving surgeries.

A single deceased donor may be able to donate kidneys, heart, lungs, liver, pancreas, and intestines, as well as a host of other tissues (some of which may be stored and used long after death). The death of one person can benefit the lives of many organ and tissue recipients in this way. Organ donations from the deaths of children are particularly important. Young children needing an organ transplant may be too small to use an adult's donated organ. The death of one child may allow several other seriously disabled children to live longer and healthier lives. The donation of organs and tissues to help improve the lives of others constitutes a remarkable form of life after death.

The End

We are born into a collection of many diverse life-forms on this planet. Our bodies, like those of other living things, are an amazing array of biological structures and biochemical functions. Throughout our lifetimes, like our fellow organisms, we must take in molecules from our surroundings to survive. Living creatures are dependent on one another, and all have their role in the natural world. As humans, we interact with our fellow beings, we accumulate knowledge and understanding, and we reproduce. However, regardless of who we are, where or how we live, what we accomplish or fail to do, from whom we came or who we leave behind, we are mortal. Everyone dies.

Although the end of a person's life can cause great sadness for his or her loved ones, life is a temporary adventure on Earth. Our human intelligence allows us to recognize death as eventual and unavoidable. Dying is an ordinary and expected part of the cycle of life. The more we know and understand about our world, the less we usually fear. Studying the science of death should be no exception. Death is part of life.

GLOSSARY

acute disorder: a medical condition that comes on suddenly

aerobic bacteria: bacteria that thrive in the presence of oxygen

algor mortis: the loss of body temperature after death

anaerobic bacteria: bacteria that live in oxygen-depleted environments

aneurysm: a weakened spot in a blood vessel wall

antidote: a chemical that will counteract a poison

arteries: vessels that carry blood away from the heart and toward body tissues

autolysis: cell rupture and digestion by a cell's own internal enzymes

autopsy: the examination of a dead body, usually to assess the cause of death

bacteria: a diverse group of single-celled life-forms with simple internal structures

biochemical: related to the chemistry of organisms

brain dead: the complete and irreversible loss of all brain function, including reflexes that control the cardiovascular and respiratory systems

cadaver: a dead body, typically intended for dissection and study

carbohydrates: organic molecules that are composed of carbon, hydrogen, and oxygen and make up various food sources, such as sugars and starches

cardiopulmonary resuscitation (CPR): a first aid method that attempts to substitute for or restart heart and respiratory functions

cardiovascular: related to the heart, vessels, and the flow of blood

cell: the smallest unit of life, consisting of a membrane that surrounds genetic material and houses living processes

chemotherapy: the medicines and other chemicals that are used to fight cancer

chronic disorder: a condition that persists over a period of time

coma: a period of unconsciousness that lasts for some duration

cremation: burning a corpse after death as a funeral rite

cryogenics: the study of the effects of extremely low temperatures on substances

cryopreservation: the use of extremely cold temperatures to prevent decomposition

decomposers: organisms that feed off decaying matter

decomposition: the changes that typically occur in an organism's body after death

DNA: deoxyribonucleic acid, the genetic material found in all life-forms

embalming: the use of chemicals to preserve a body after death

entomologists: scientists who study insects

enzyme: a protein that aids in a specific chemical reaction

euthanasia: the act of ending the life of a person with a terminal illness

forensic: related to the law and open for legal interpretation

fungi: a kingdom of organisms that decompose decaying matter

genetic disease: a condition resulting from faulty DNA that can be passed from parent to offspring

homeostasis: an organism's control of necessary body conditions at specific levels or in a relatively constant range

hormone: a body chemical that regulates the functions of cells and organs

immune system: the combination of cells, tissues, and organs that helps the body ward off infection

livor mortis: the pooling of blood that occurs in a body after death

malignant tumor: a cancerous mass that can spread to other tissues

medicolegal: combining aspects of law and medicine

metabolism: the sum of all the chemical reactions occurring within a living organism

metamorphosis: a set of dramatic physical changes that takes place in some animals, such as insects

microorganisms: bacteria and other life-forms too small to be seen without magnification

mummification: the process of drying out a body, which preserves it from decomposition

necrophagous: describes organisms that eat dead flesh

organ: a collection of different types of tissues that forms a specific structure in the body

organelle: small organs contained within cells that have specific structure and function

organ transplant: moving an organ or part of an organ from one person to another

orifices: body openings that lead to internal cavities or passageways

pathologist: a person, usually a medical doctor, who studies disease

postmortem period: the time after death

prognosis: the expected course or outcome of a disorder or disease

protists: a diverse group of life-forms that consists primarily of single-celled organisms

radiation therapy: the use of energy sources to fight cancer

reflex: a fast, involuntary, and predictable body response to a change in the internal or external environment

rigor mortis: muscle rigidity that occurs after death

scavengers: organisms that feed on dead flesh

shock: the inability of the cardiovascular system to deliver oxygen and nutrients to tissues

stem cell: an immature or undifferentiated cell that retains the capacity to develop into a variety of other cell types

system: a collection of related organs that works together toward a set of body functions

taphonomy: the study of the environmental influences that act upon an organism after death

tissue: a group of related cells, usually forming a layer within the body

toxicologists: scientists who study the effects of harmful chemicals on life-forms

toxins: chemical poisons capable of damaging tissue

trauma: a stressful event that results in one or more injuries to the body

vegetative state: an altered state of consciousness in which a person retains some basic body reflexes and even appears awake at times but is not responsive to the environment

viruses: nonliving pieces of genetic material and protein that can enter cells and cause disease

BIBLIOGRAPHY

Dix, Jay, and Michael Graham. *Time of Death, Decomposition and Identification: An Atlas*. Boca Raton, FL: CRC Press, 2000.

Dunning, Arend. "Lessons from the Dead." *New Scientist Magazine*, January 30, 1993, 44–47.

Haglund, William D., and Marcella H. Sorg. *Advances in Forensic Taphonomy*. Boca Raton, FL: CRC Press, 2002.

———. *Forensic Taphonomy: The Postmortem Fate of Human Remains*. Boca Raton, FL: CRC Press, 1997.

Hanzlick, Randy. *Death Investigation: Systems and Procedures*. Boca Raton, FL: CRC Press, 2007.

Hospice of North Central Florida. *Preparing for Approaching Death*. 1996. http://www.hospicenet.org/html/preparing_for-pr.html (February 1, 2009).

Iserson, Kenneth V. *Death to Dust: What Happens to Dead Bodies*. Tucson: Galen Press, 1994.

Kerrigan, Michael. *The History of Death*. London: Amber Books, 2007.

Knight, Bernard. *Simpson's Forensic Medicine*. 11th ed. London: Arnold, 1997.

Kumar, Vinay, Ramzi S. Cotran, and Stanley L. Robbins. *Basic Pathology*. 6th ed. Philadelphia: W. B. Saunders Company, 1997.

Lyle, D. P. *Murder and Mayhem: A Doctor Answers Medical and Forensic Questions*. New York: Thomas Dunne-St. Martin's Press, 2003.

Micozzi, Marc S. *Postmortem Change in Human and Animal Remains*. Springfield, IL: Charles C. Thomas, 1991.

Nuland, Sherwin B. *How We Die: Reflections on Life's Final Chapter*. New York: Vintage, 1993.

Perry, Jerome J., James T. Staley, and Stephen Lory. *Microbial Life*. Sunderland, MA: Sinauer Associates, 2002.

President's Commission for the Study of Ethical Problems in Medicine and Biomedical and Behavioral Research. *Defining Death: A Report on the Medical, Legal and Ethical Issues in the Determination of Death.* Washington, DC: U.S. Government Printing Office, 1981.

Raven, Peter H., George B. Johnson, Jonathan B. Losos, and Susan R. Singer. *Biology.* 7th ed. New York: McGraw-Hill, 2005.

Ribowsky, Shiya. *Dead Center: Behind the Scenes at the World's Largest Medical Examiner's Office.* New York: HarperCollins, 2006.

Roach, Mary. *Stiff: The Curious Lives of Human Cadavers.* New York: Norton and Company, 2003.

Sachs, Jessica Snyder. *Corpse: Nature, Forensics, and the Struggle to Pinpoint the Time of Death.* Cambridge, MA: Basic Books, 2001.

Tortora, Gerald J., and Bryan Derrickson. *Principles of Anatomy and Physiology.* 11th ed. Hoboken, NJ: Wiley, 2006.

U.S. Department of Health and Human Services. *Organ Procurement and Transplantation Network.* 2009. http://optn.transplant.hrsa.gov/ (May 30, 2009).

FURTHER READING

Books

Bass, Bill, and Jon Jefferson. *Death's Acre*. New York: Berkley Books, 2003.

Dobson, Mary. *Disease: The Extraordinary Stories behind History's Deadliest Killers*. Cambridge, UK: Quercus, 2007.

Fridell, Ron. *Decoding Life: Unraveling the Mysteries of the Genome*. Minneapolis: Twenty-First Century Books, 2005.

Friedlander, Mark P., Jr. *Outbreak: Disease Detectives at Work*. Minneapolis: Twenty-First Century Books, 2009.

Friedlander, Mark P., Jr., and Terry Phillips. *When Objects Talk: Solving a Crime with Science*. Minneapolis: Twenty-First Century Books, 2001.

Greene, Meg. *Rest in Peace*. Minneapolis: Twenty-First Century Books, 2008.

Largo, Michael. *Final Exits: The Illustrated Encyclopedia of How We Die*. New York: HarperCollins, 2006.

Walker, Sally M. *Written in Bone: Buried Lives of Jamestown and Colonial Maryland*. Minneapolis: Carolrhoda Books, 2009.

Winner, Cherie. *Circulating Life: Blood Transfusion from Ancient Superstition to Modern Medicine*. Minneapolis: Twenty-First Century Books, 2007.

———. *Cryobiology*. Minneapolis: Lerner Publications Company, 2006.

Websites

Advance Directives and Do Not Resuscitate Orders
http://familydoctor.org/online/famdocen/home/pat-advocacy/endoflife/003.html
Learn more about living wills and other end-of-life directives.

American Board of Forensic Entomology
http://www.forensicentomologist.org/index.html
Case studies explain how forensic entomologists use insects to determine the time of death.

American Board of Medicolegal Death Investigation
http://medschool.slu.edu/abmdi/index.php
This site has information about death investigation standards and certification.

Ask Dr. Baden
http://www.hbo.com/autopsy/baden/qa_1.html
  Questions and answers about autopsy are presented here.

Australian Museum
http://www.deathonline.net/decomposition/index.htm
  Photos and text at this site introduce the stages of decomposition.

Cells Alive
http://www.cellsalive.com/index.htm
  Interactive diagrams show the workings of different kinds of cells.

Decay and Decomposition
http://uk.encarta.msn.com/encyclopedia_781532796/decay_and
_decomposition.html
  Decomposition and decay are explained at this site.

Hospice Foundation of America
http://www.hospicefoundation.org/endOfLifeInfo/myths_dying.asp
  This is a list of facts and myths, with explanations, about dying.

Just Dying to Get Out
http://www.snopes.com/horrors/gruesome/buried.asp
  Stories of people being buried alive appear here.

Physiological Homeostasis
http://www.biology-online.org/4/1_physiological_homeostasis.htm
  This site gives examples of how homeostasis works in the human body.

Rader's Biology 4 Kids.com
http://www.biology4kids.com/files/systems_main.html
  Text and diagrams explain body systems and tissues.

University of Tennessee's Department of Anthropology
http://web.utk.edu/~fac/
  This is the history of the Body Farm and how its research aids in identification
  and investigation of human remains.

U.S. Centers for Disease Control and Prevention
http://www.cdc.gov/
  Articles on all aspects of health, disease, injuries, and emergency medicine are
  provided here.

INDEX

ABOUT THE AUTHOR

Dr. Elizabeth Murray has been an educator and a forensic scientist for over twenty years. Her primary teaching focus is human anatomy and physiology. She is one of about sixty-five anthropologists certified as an expert by the American Board of Forensic Anthropology. Dr. Murray was scientific consultant and on-camera personality for the miniseries *Skeleton Crew* for the National Geographic Channel and a regular cast member on the Discovery Health Channel series *Skeleton Stories*.

PHOTO ACKNOWLEDGMENTS

The images in this book are used with permission of: © S. Lowry/Univ Ulster/Stone/Getty Images, pp. 2, 7, 15, 33, 45, 57, 69, 89, 102, 104, 106, 108, 110, 112; © iStockphoto. com/Carmen Martínez Banús, p. 6; © Laura Westlund/Independent Picture Service, pp. 9, 11, 18; © Steve Gschmeissner/SPL/Getty Images, p. 12; © ALIX/Photo Researchers, Inc., p. 14; © Medical RF/The Medical File/Peter Arnold, Inc., p. 17; © Dr. Elizabeth A. Murray, pp. 19, 22, 25, 31, 46, 61, 62, 70, 91, 92, 95; © Ed Reschke/Peter Arnold, Inc., p. 21; © Zephyr/Photo Researchers, Inc., p. 24; © Rubberball/Getty Images, p. 29; © Enigma/Alamy, p. 32; Paul Gunning/Photo Researchers, Inc., p. 34; © iStockphoto.com/ Sean Locke, p. 35; © Charlie Neuman/San Diego Union-Tribune/ZUMA Press, p. 36; © Simon Fraser/Royal Victoria Infirmary, Newcastle/Photo Researchers, Inc., p. 41; SIU BIOMED COMM/Custom Medical Stock Photo, p. 44; © Ed Kashi/CORBIS, p. 47; Library of Congress (LC-USZ62-118008), p. 51; © Tim Boyles/Getty Images, p. 54; © BSIP, Laurent/CL. H. AMERIC/Photo Researchers, Inc., p. 55; © Medicimage/The Medical File/Peter Arnold, Inc., p. 56; © Peter Menzel/Photo Researchers, Inc., p. 58; © Dean Lewins/EPA/CORBIS, p. 64; © Bettmann/CORBIS, p. 68; © Volker Steger/ Photo Researchers, Inc., pp. 72, 81 (right); © Howard Sochurek/The Medical File/Peter Arnold, Inc., p. 77; © Image Quest 3-D/NHPA/Photoshot, p. 81 (left); © David Howells/ CORBIS, p. 83; Kevin Beebe/Custom Medical Stock Photo, p. 84; © Reza/Webistan/ CORBIS, p. 86; © Hector Mata/AFP/Getty Images, p. 88; © Michelle Del Guercio/The Medical File/Peter Arnold, Inc., p. 94; © World History/Topham/The Image Works, p. 96, © Phototake Inc./Alamy, p. 100.

Front cover: © Costantino Margiotta/Photo Researchers, Inc. (top); © Dennis Kunkel Microscopy, Inc./PHOTOTAKE/Alamy (bottom). Back cover: © S. Lowry/Univ Ulster/ Stone/Getty Images (jacket).